# ANGER MASTERY

## Also by Kevin B. Burk

*Astrology: Understanding the Birth Chart*

*The Complete Node Book*

*The Relationship Handbook:*
*How to Understand and Improve Every Relationship*
*in Your Life*

*The Relationship Workbook:*
*How to Understand and Improve Every Relationship*
*in Your Life*

*Astrology Math Made Easy*

*The Relationship Workbook:*
*How to Design and Create Your Ideal Romantic*
*Relationship*

*The Relationship Workbook:*
*The Secrets of Successful Team Building*

*Astrological Relationship Handbook:*
*How to Use Astrology to Understand Every Relationship*
*in Your Life*

*Astrological Relationship Workbook:*
*How to Use Astrology to Understand Every Relationship*
*in Your Life*

*Astrology & The Law of Attraction*

# ANGER
# MASTERY

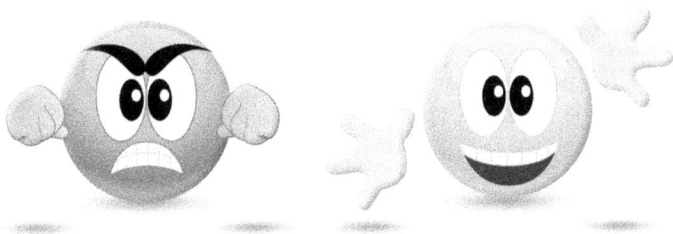

## Get Angry, Get Happy

### by
# Kevin B. Burk

SERENDIPITY
P·R·E·S·S
LA MESA, CALIFORNIA

ISBN 978-0-9759682-3-9

Printed in the United States of America.

Published by
Serendipity Press
La Mesa, California

Book design and cover design by Kevin B. Burk.

For Jon Stewart,
with thanks (in advance)

# Acknowledgments & Appreciation

**W**riting is very much a collaborative process, although in my case, most of my collaborators don't know that they're collaborating with me. I find inspiration in the strangest places, and more than once, an off-hand question or comment has prompted a profound change in the focus of a work in progress.

I do find myself in a slight quandary, however. While there are many people whom I would like to thank for their often unintentional contributions to this book, I'm not sure they would appreciate being recognized for contributing to a book on anger. So I'll just thank my family, and leave it at that.

I can, however, thank the individuals who actively participated in making this book possible. Most of those individuals are members of my spiritual community, Universal Spirit Center in San Diego, and without the love and support of that community, this book wouldn't exist. Michele Mathieu, Kathryn Huff, Kristen Johnson and Jeffrey Stasny caught typos and provided valuable feedback, as did my parents Bernard and Barbara Burk.

This book contains many of the core concepts that came into form during the three and a half years I was working on what would eventually become *Astrology & The Law of Attraction*. I'm grateful to all of my students and clients who allowed me to share and refine this material. I'm also grateful to the Gulf Coast Chapter of NCGR, the San Diego Astrological Society (SDAS), the Southern California Astrological Network (SCAN), the Fraser Valley Astrological Guild, and the Oregon Astrological Association, all of whom invited me to share this work in progress with their members.

I also want to thank Wade Mayberry and Eric Slovin. While they didn't play an active role in the creation of this book, they are helping with the marketing and promotion, so I'm thanking them in advance.

But most of all, I would like to thank Claudia Previn Stasny. Not only has Claudia been my weekly sounding-board (and spiritual support) through the creation process of two books and at least three classes, but Claudia also functioned as my *de facto* editor, going through every word of the book, catching typos and grammatical inconsistencies. Claudia is a fabulous editor, and any unconventional grammar or strange capitalization you may find in the finished book are conscious, deliberate choices on my part. Of course, she didn't see this section because I wanted to surprise her, so their maybe a fEw isues or typoggraphical errors that I;ll have to fix in the next edition.

# ANGER MASTERY

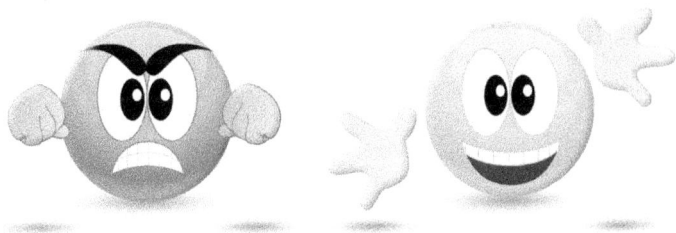

# INTRODUCTION

# Chapter 1
# Welcome to the Matrix

Good morning. This is your wake-up call.

It's time for you to make a choice: the Red Pill or the Blue Pill. If you choose the Red Pill, your life will never be the same. You will wake up and face the reality of how unhappy you are. However, you will also learn what you can do about it, and receive the tools that you can use to become truly happy. If you choose the Blue Pill, you'll go on with your life and continue to believe whatever you choose to believe.

Make your choice and take your pill now.

Ok. I'll admit, this worked a lot better in *The Matrix*. For one thing, in *The Matrix* there were actual pills. I wanted to include real pills with this book, but you wouldn't believe how much that was going to cost. Instead, you'll have to make do with virtual pills.

If you chose the Blue Pill, you're finished with this book. Why don't you go back and re-read the Harry Potter series? (They're classics, and they hold up.)

If you chose the Red Pill, keep reading. It's time to wake up and smell the coffee.[1]

It's time you put aside your fantasies about winning the lottery or becoming famous, or having the perfect body, and wake up to

---

[1] The coffee is also virtual.

your reality. This will not be a pleasant awakening, because your reality is pretty awful. Life is a constant struggle. No matter how hard you work, things are not improving. You have more stress and less money today than you did a year ago. You're not happy. You haven't been happy for so long that you don't know what happy is anymore. And worst of all, you don't have enough energy to do anything about it.

The reason you don't have enough energy to improve your life is that other people are stealing it from you.

This might surprise you. After all, you would never let someone siphon gas from your car or steal your electricity. And yet, every single day, you let other people steal the most important energy you have. The more energy they steal from you, the more you struggle, and the harder your life gets; and the harder your life gets, the more you struggle, and the more energy they steal from you.

This energy is more vital and more useful than gas or electricity. You don't even realize how important this energy is. And as long as you remain ignorant of how to control and channel this energy, other people will steal it from you and make you a victim.

Does this make you mad? Good! Because the energy I'm talking about is anger, and when you learn how to master your anger, you can avoid ever being a victim again.

Your anger is very powerful. Your anger can help you to get everything you want. Ultimately your anger can help you to become truly happy. But first, you have to learn to master your anger. If you don't master your anger, it will master you, and you will continue to be victimized and manipulated. You will waste more energy, and feel less happy. In other words, your life will continue exactly as it is now.

# Why Master Your Anger?

Mastering your anger is important, because when you master your anger, it will be harder to manipulate you. Anger is an emotion. When you get emotional, you stop thinking clearly, and you're far more likely to say and do things that you will regret later. This is why it's so easy to manipulate angry people into believing, saying, and doing things they would never consider in a rational state of mind.

Anger is like fire: it's a powerful source of energy, but you have to know how to control it. When you consciously direct the energy of your anger, it becomes a positive, creative force in your life that can help you to become truly happy. If you don't consciously direct the energy of your anger, it becomes dangerous and destructive. Anger can lead to aggression, rage and violence. If you don't give it an outlet, it can cause severe, debilitating depression. Either way, it turns you into a weak, impotent victim, and allows other people to steal your energy and your power.

By the time you finish reading this book, you'll understand the reasons why all of this is true. More importantly, by the time you finish reading this book, it will be much harder for other people to manipulate you and steal your energy.

Of course, if you do more than just read this book—if you actually follow the Anger Mastery Process and do the work—you'll gain control over your life, and finally be happy.

Before any of this can happen, though, you have to wake up and face the reality of your life. You have to face the fact that most of the time you're angry, afraid, and miserable. Before you can take back your power, you have to accept the fact that right now, you are a victim. Every day, other people are stealing your power and energy from you.

## Shall We Play a Game?

You've spent most of your life playing a game. When you first chose to play this game, you didn't know all of the rules, but you played anyway, because all the cool kids were playing it. This game is about money and power. The objective of the game is to get as much money (and power) as possible. In this game, there's a fixed and limited supply of money, so the only way to get money is to take it away from other players. How much money you can get is determined by how much money you have: the more you have, the more you can get. The only way to win the game is to get *all* of the money.

You don't care about money or power; what you care about is happiness. You play the game because you believe that when you get enough money or power, then you'll be happy. This, however, is a lie. Happiness is not a part of this game.

You are barely a pawn in this game. As long as you play this game, you will be a victim. Other people will control and manipulate you to further their own agenda. Other players will lie to you to keep you invested in the game, so they can steal your money and your power. You have absolutely no chance of winning this game. The only way to win this game is not to play.

The good news is that you don't have to keep playing this game. When you learn how to master your anger, you can stop playing it, and no one will be able to steal your power anymore.

Before you can do that, however, you need to meet the people who are running the game. They control this world. Whether you know it or not, as long as you play this game, you're enslaved to them. They steal your energy, your money, and your happiness. They use politicians, governments and the media to manipulate, brainwash and distract you. These are the people behind the curtain: *The Rich*.

You don't know any of *The Rich*. You've never met them, you've never seen them, and you've never heard of them. They don't show up on any lists of the world's wealthiest people. But make no mistake: they control every aspect of this game of money and power, including the lives of everyone who chooses to play the game.

These people aren't just wealthy. They're not just filthy rich. Billionaires aren't even in their league. When these people are short a few million dollars, they find it in their sofa cushions. They're not just rich, they're *The Rich*. They merit the fancy typeface. In fact, they own it.

*The Rich* aren't mere bankers; they're the ones that create and maintain the illusion of money itself. They deal in *finance* and *economics* and, on the whole, they treat them like a global game of three-card monte. They control every media outlet in the world. They control every government in the world. And no matter how much money, power, control and influence they have, it's never enough. They won't be satisfied until they have all of it.

*The Rich* have been putting their agenda in place for hundreds of years. The way that *The Rich* manage to steal your money and get you to further their agenda is by keeping you scared, angry and stupid. If you ever started to think for yourself, *The Rich* wouldn't be able to steal your power. Sadly, there's little danger of that. Not only have Americans become increasingly stupid and arrogant over the past few decades, on the whole, Americans are *proud* of how stupid and arrogant we are.

Everyone in the media has an agenda. Everyone in the media is trying to manipulate you. Most of the time that agenda is to keep you scared and angry, because scared and angry people will do *anything* if they think it will help them to feel Safe. If people are scared and angry enough, they can even be manipulated into acting against their own best interest. Angry and scared people aren't just sheep; they're lambs who fight to be the first inside the slaughterhouse.

I'm sure you believe that none of this applies to you. You're probably confident in your ability to see through the lies and the misdirection, and uncover the truth. *The Rich* love people like you.

But let me demonstrate to you how you've been manipulated and misdirected. Let's go back to the issue of money and consider the U.S. National Debt. As I start typing this sentence, the U.S. National Debt is $14,287,400,910,973. When I finished typing that sentence, the U.S. National Debt had climbed to $14,287,401,870,990. That's over $14 *trillion* dollars (and counting) that we owe as a country.

You're probably aware of the great debates caused by this mounting debt. You may wonder who's responsible for it. It's a fact, after all, that the wars that Bush started in the Middle East have added billions to the debt. It's also a fact that the Bush tax cuts for the wealthy have also made it worse. You might believe that the real issue is that the government spends too much money, and that the solution to the debt crisis is to cut spending and tighten our belts. You might believe that we have to raise taxes to close the deficit gap. You might ask how the debt is hurting the economy. You might wonder what impact it has on jobs and unemployment. You might ask what it's doing to the stock market.

However, there's one question that you never think to ask, and the purpose of all of the debates and arguments and finger pointing is to stop you from asking it:

### *Who the hell do we owe $14 trillion to?*[2]

The fact is that we owe the $14 trillion (and counting) to the Central Bank of the Federal Reserve. They're very invested in your not knowing that, or at least not understanding what that means, because the Central Bank and the Federal Reserve are controlled by *The Rich*.

The Federal Reserve Board is a group of bankers who have taken over the ability to regulate and create money from the United States Treasury. It is not a government agency. It is a private organization, and it has never, ever been audited or investigated by the U.S. Congress. There is no government oversight of the Federal Reserve. And the Federal Reserve Board, effectively, owns the entire country.

Now, I encourage you to verify everything—including everything that I tell you here. However, I should warn you that doing research on the Federal Reserve can be tricky. About half of the information you'll find is dense and boring enough that it's a drug-free cure for insomnia. The other half of the information you'll find is thrilling and exciting. It's so vivid, in fact, that you can almost hear the crackle of the author's tin-foil

[2] This question, I know, has a host of grammatical errors. Technically, it should be "To whom the hell do we owe $14 trillion?" but that's almost as stupid as actually owing more than $14 trillion and not knowing to whom the hell we owe it.

hat as the CIA's mind-control rays bounce off of it. The truth lies somewhere in the middle. All you really need to understand about the members of the Federal Reserve Board is that they're running the game. You don't need to know how they do it or why. When you stop playing the game, it no longer matters.

## A Fairly Balanced Reply

In the interest of being "Fairly Balanced[3]," I'm giving *The Rich* a chance to state their case.

> America is the greatest country in the world. And do you know what makes it so great? We do. *The Rich*. We are the American Dream—the idea that one day, if you work hard enough, you too could become one of *The Rich*.
>
> But so few people appreciate us for all of the good we do. We hold lavish, fancy benefits and raise other people's money for good causes. And of course, we work tirelessly to change the laws and regulations so that we can keep all of our money when we make it— and we do it all for you. Sure, those tax cuts for the wealthy have made life a little harder for some people, but when your lottery numbers finally hit, and you cash that big check, you'll thank us.
>
> We're *The Rich*, and we care. We're looking after your best interests.
>
> Oh, who—or more pretentiously, *whom*—the hell am I kidding? I know that's all a heaping load of crap, and so

---

[3] The term "Fairly Balanced" does not infringe on any existing trademark or copyright of any media organization. So take that, Foxy Newts.

do you. But you know what's so great? Even though it's a heaping load of crap, you're still willing to buy it.

Would you compromise your morals and ethics, take away the rights of others, undermine the foundation of the U.S. Constitution, and ultimately limit your own freedom for $100 million and a private jet? What about for $20 and a coupon for Netflix?

Hey, there's no need to get all huffy. We've already established that you're a cowardly, opportunistic, short-sighted whore. Now, we're just negotiating price.

Look at the world today. Integrity, self-respect, compassion and altruism are on the endangered species list. It's gotten so easy (not to mention cheap) to control you that it almost takes all of the fun out of it. I mean, when we can convince almost half of the country that affordable, available, quality health care is a *bad* thing, and get them to fight tooth and nail for the right to give *more* money to the private insurance companies that we control, what do we do for an encore?

We don't even have to hide in the shadows anymore because you're too weak to stop us. We just finished causing the biggest financial crisis since the Great Depression. We gobbled up your savings, your retirement, and your pensions, and what did you do? You gave us billions in tax dollars for dessert. Now that you're working two jobs and still not making ends met, you don't even have enough energy left to complain.

We've almost completely eliminated the so-called "middle class." We've taken your anger and manipulated you into gutting every social program that supports the poor. You're too stupid to realize that it's only a matter of time until *you'll* be poor and wishing those programs were there to help you and your family. And once we've sucked up all of your money, we'll go after the "wealthy" and the "upper class." They're so stupid that they won't see us coming until it's too late.

It's never been "trickle-down" economics. It's always been "trickle-*up*." All of the money, wealth and resources of the world are flowing up to the very top where they belong. Soon, we'll have it all. Soon, we'll own everything and everyone in the world. And *then*, we'll finally be happy.

If you don't like it, why don't you switch off your television and go read a book? Yeah, that's what I thought! I bet you don't even have the backbone to finish reading *this* book.

God, I love this country. I wonder how much China would pay for it?

## **My Unhidden Agenda**

As I said earlier, *everyone* in the media has an agenda. Everyone in the media is trying to manipulate you into doing something. Most of the time, they're interested in siphoning the energy of your anger to support their own agendas.

Now, it may occur to you that as an author and a speaker, I am also, technically, a part of the media, and that would be correct. I am a part of the media, and I do have an agenda. The big difference is that my agenda is spelled out for you right here:

## 1. Money

I'd like to have some of yours. If you're reading this, chances are, I've already got some of your money because you bought this book. (Thank you!) Because I'm both the author and the publisher, a reasonable percentage of the $9.95 you spent on the book went directly into my bank accounts. This book is printed on-demand, and the print cost per book averages around $3. If you bought the book from a retailer like Amazon.com, I made about $3.50 (before taxes). If you bought the book directly from me, I made about $6.50 (before taxes). Again, thank you. I'll do my best to give you at least your money's worth.

## 2. Reduce the Amount of Suffering in the World

In my own small way, my life is dedicated to reducing the amount of optional suffering in the world. This is why I write my books. This is why I teach my classes and workshops. And this is why I work with clients one-on-one.

This process is more challenging than it sounds because the way that I avoid suffering in my own life is to live my life in absolute integrity. This means that I do my best to stay within the boundaries of "My Business," and not get involved in "Other People's Business," or "God's Business." (This will make more sense when you get to Chapter 4.)

I'm aware of the tremendous increase in suffering in the world, and in particular in the United States, because that's where I live. I've observed the epidemic of bad behavior, and the absence of civility in politics, and I'm disturbed by the amount of hate and bile that I see festering everywhere I look. I'm amazed and appalled at how so many people in this country have been manipulated, brainwashed, and programmed into acting against their own best interests time and again. I notice all of this, and I get angry, and I realize that this is none of my business.

I know this is none of my business because I have no interest in politics. I am not called to public service, and I will never run for office. Because of that, there's nothing that I can do to influence or change what appears to be the cause of these problems.

The reason that you're suffering and being manipulated, victimized and abused is that you don't know how to master the power of your anger. I've been there myself, and I know what it's like. Over the course of many years, I learned how to master my own anger, take back my power, and become truly happy. What I *can* do is share with you how I did it. And I can do this while staying within the boundaries of "My Business."

It's none of my business what you do with this information. I do believe, however, that some people will use it to take back their power. I believe that some people will choose to become personally responsible for their lives, and begin to think for themselves. I believe that those people will become happier, and as a result, there will be a little less suffering in the world.

I'm not interested in changing your opinions, or your politics. Your opinions and politics are none of my business. But I am hoping to be able to manipulate you, and challenge you, and inspire you so that you begin to question your reality and take back some of your power.

# The Anger Mastery Process

The Anger Mastery Process has three phases.

**Phase 1** has two objectives. First, you'll develop your ability to process more energy. It's so easy for *The Rich* to siphon off your power because you can't handle it. In Phase 1, you'll learn how to use and direct more of your own energy. Second, you'll learn how to reclaim your power, step out of Victim Consciousness, and move into integrity.

In **Phase 2**, you'll learn how to transform your relationship with anger by developing your safety muscles and maintaining a healthy balance in your Safety Need Account. This will help you to stay out of Victim Consciousness. By the end of Phase 2, when you feel angry, you'll be able to *respond*, instead of to *react*.

Finally, in **Phase 3**, you'll learn how to channel and direct the energy of your anger in ways that are creative, supportive and powerful. You'll learn how to break free of the values and social expectations that have kept you trapped in Victim Consciousness, and you'll discover your own, individual path to happiness.

# You Have to Do the Work!

If you want to change your life, you can't just read about how to do it. You actually have to do the work. If reading was enough to change your life, you'd be rich, thin, and have the sex drive of a teenager.

Mastering your anger is a *process*, not an *event*. And it won't be enough to go through the process just once. If you truly want to be happy, you'll have to keep applying the tools for the rest of your life.

Whether you do the work or not is none of my business. It's also none of my concern. I've already got some of your money (thank you!), and it doesn't matter to me if you choose to give away your power, be manipulated, and have your life drain away. That just makes you an ordinary person.

But perhaps you're not just an ordinary person. Perhaps you truly want to change your life and become happy. The challenge is that wanting to change your life and actually being able to change it are two different things. You're stuck in your life. You've been lied to, and abused, and beaten down, and brainwashed so that you don't question the way things are, and you don't have enough energy to do anything about it. If you want to break out of this trap, you need a lot of energy. That's why I've been doing my best to make you angry! The energy of your anger is how you can begin to take back your power. But you have to get angry enough so that you get your butt off the couch, turn off the television and the computer, and actually *do* something. And you have to *keep* doing it in order to break out of the prison of your life.

So what are you waiting for? Get up off the couch and *do something!* Go to the gym and work out!

Seriously. I'm not kidding.

Going to the gym and working out is the most important part of Phase 1. But don't take my word for it. Read all about it in Chapter 2.[4]

---

[4] Yes, technically, when you read Chapter 2, you'll still be taking my word for it; however, you'll be taking my word for it in a different chapter. And face it—you've already paid for the book. You might as well get your money's worth.

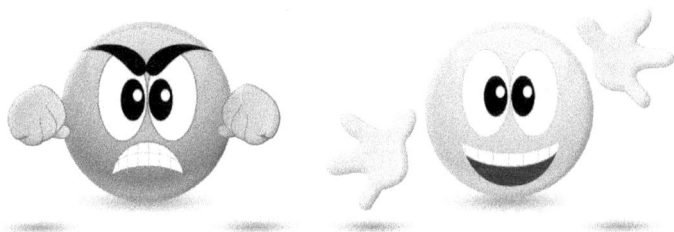

# ANGER MASTERY

## PHASE 1

# Chapter 2
# Working Out Your Anger

**E**very day, people are stealing your energy and taking your power, and you can't stop them. Do you want your power? You think you're entitled to your power? **You want your power?** *Well, you can't handle your power!* [1]

Seriously. You *literally* can't handle your power. It's time for the truth. (You may not be able to handle your power, but you *can* handle the truth). Not only can you not stop *The Rich* and their minions from stealing your power and using it for their own agendas, but you *need* them to steal it from you. Right now, you're like a 120-volt appliance plugged into a 240-volt outlet. If they didn't steal your power, it would fry your circuits.

You're always looking for ways to get rid of this excess energy, because this excess energy is incredibly painful. Some people numb themselves to the pain by stuffing with food; others get drunk, smoke, or do drugs. Some people bleed off their excess energy with sex; others do it with gambling. Some people go shopping, wasting energy by spending money; others use this energy to create a fantasy world, losing themselves in video games or computers.

In small doses, these activities are not destructive; however, when they are pursued to excess, they are detrimental to your

---

[1] This will be a lot more effective in the audio book. I'm hoping to hire Jack Nicholson to read this chapter.

health, your life, and your happiness. You become addicted to these behaviors. The more energy you give to them, the less energy you can use yourself—which means you have to give even more energy to your addictions and distractions.

In order to reclaim your power, you first have to be able to use it. You have to train yourself to channel and process increasing amounts of energy. You don't have to give up any of the activities that you enjoy (which you're using to bleed off your excess energy). When you master your own energy, you can choose to spend some of it on these activities. The difference is that it will be your choice.

It's only a two-step process to increase the amount of energy that you can handle:

1.  Get a gym membership.
2.  Use it at least five times a week.

Before I go any further, let me cover all of the necessary legal disclaimers. See a doctor or a qualified medical professional before you start any exercise regimen—especially if you've been living a sedentary life, or have any health challenges. You may not be physically able to go work out at the gym right now. However, no matter what your physical condition, there will be *something* you can do that will expend energy and raise your heart rate. Over time, this will help you to take control of your life and move out of Victim Consciousness. If you're completely new to the concept of physical exercise, find a trainer to work with you. Not only will a trainer help keep you motivated, but he or she will also help you reduce the risk of injury.

# No Pain, No Gain (No Kidding)

The only way to get any results and to make any progress is to work outside of your comfort zone. This doesn't mean that you have to push yourself to the breaking point (please don't!), but it does mean that you have to push yourself past your limits—or at least what you think your limits are.

The old motto, "no pain, no gain" applies, albeit with some important clarifications. You should not experience any *physical* pain when you are exercising. If something hurts when you're working out, *stop*. You should never experience any sharp pain in your body. You may, however, experience stiffness and soreness because you haven't developed your muscles yet. If that's what you're experiencing, get over it. Continue with your workout, as long as you don't experience any sharp physical pain.

You may also experience a certain amount of *emotional* pain. Deal with it. This is the pain that you have to suck up and plow through. You need to learn to ignore the voice in your head that tells you that you can't do the full 20 minutes on the treadmill, or that you're too tired to go to the gym at all. With some dedication and practice, you can shut that voice up. That voice is the voice you hear when you give up your power and step into Victim Consciousness. It's not your friend.

When you are ready to begin a daily exercise program as part of Phase 1 of the Anger Mastery Process, it's essential that you *not* set any weight loss or fitness goals. This is not about helping you to fit into your skinny jeans. This is not the "Anger Diet." Don't make any radical changes to your eating habits. Don't weigh yourself. Don't measure yourself. And don't look at yourself naked in the mirror.

I'll bet you weren't expecting to hear *that*.

It's important that you follow these instructions, however, because if you set any fitness goals when you begin the Anger Mastery Process, you will fail. You won't reach your goals, you won't continue the Anger Mastery Process, and you won't get happy. In Chapter 3, I'll explain why this is true, but for now, just trust me. This is not about getting into shape or losing weight. This is about increasing your ability to handle energy so you can become happy.

When you start exercising at least five times a week, always working outside of your comfort zone, will you see changes in your physical body? Probably. You may also find that you naturally make different food choices as you settle into this new routine. The point is, until you've mastered the first two phases of the Anger Mastery Process, do not incorporate fitness or weight-loss goals into your exercise program. Focus on using up your own energy for its own sake. Once you've moved on to Phase 3, you can set whatever fitness goals you like—and you'll have a much easier time achieving them.

It doesn't matter what kind of exercise you do, as long as it raises your heart rate and makes you sweat. If you've been living the typical American sedentary lifestyle, start with walking. The first day, you may be able to walk for only 10 minutes. That's your baseline. The next day, walk a little farther. Keep working just outside of your comfort zone. You will gradually be able to do more, and eventually you can try more intense kinds of exercise.

Martial arts are especially effective in channeling the energy of anger. You have a full spectrum to choose from, ranging from the "softer" forms like Tai Chi and Qigong, to the "harder," more active and aggressive forms like Karate and Akido. Martial arts specifically train you to access, focus, channel and control your energy. They can provide powerful, healthy outlets for you to direct and manage your anger.

# Get Angry, Get Moving

Phase 1 of the Anger Mastery Process is not only about learning how to channel and use more of your energy. It's also about becoming conscious of the energy of your anger, and learning to use it in positive, supportive ways. Your daily (or almost daily) exercise routine helps to burn off some of the stored energy you carry around with you. But when you get angry, you can't always drop everything and head to the gym.

The most important thing to know right now about the energy of anger is that you don't have to use that energy to lash out at whatever or whoever triggered your anger. It's your energy, and you can use it constructively. Anger can give you a temporary boost of focus and determination. Take advantage of this, and do some of the things you know you need to do, but you never get around to doing. Clean out the garage. Do the dishes. File your taxes. Mow the lawn.

At this point, it's best to focus on simple, direct activities that don't involve interactions with other people. Avoid venting your frustration or telling your story out loud. You can let your list of grievances play out in the comfort and safety of your own head, while you use that extra boost of energy to cross things off your To Do list. As you become more skilled in the Anger Mastery Process, you'll be able to use this energy to accomplish more meaningful and long-term goals.

## Stick With the Process

If you stop reading here and all you get out of this book is the inspiration to exercise at least five times a week, always working just outside of your comfort zone, over time you will experience an increase in your happiness. When I say "over time," I don't mean you'll notice any profound changes during the first week. I can't even promise you'll see improvements during the first month. But if you stick with the process, you will begin to experience not only the benefits of better health through physical fitness, but also the benefits of less undirected anger.

If you want to see *real* results, keep reading. The biggest and the fastest transformations happen when you incorporate all three phases of the Anger Mastery Process. But I can't emphasize enough how important the gym membership is. You *must* train yourself to be able to use more of your own energy, and you must begin to burn off the stored anger you're carrying around with you.

The gym I belong to is very supportive of this. I spend most of my time at the gym on the elliptical cross trainer machines. At my gym, these machines face rows of televisions that are usually tuned to CNN, MSNBC or FOX News. Anytime I start to feel tired in the middle of my workout, all I have to do is look up, and I get a fresh burst of anger that helps me power through the rest of my workout. It's better than Red Bull.

## What's Next?

The next chapter is incredibly important. It creates the context for you to understand the true nature of anger, and how you can use that energy to get happy. It explores (and questions) the nature of reality. And it explains what I mean when I talk about Victim Consciousness.

As I said, it's incredibly important. It also contains some of the most challenging concepts that you'll find in this book.

When you first read Chapter 3, read it slowly. Take in whatever you can. You don't have to completely understand (or even believe) it. As long as you "get" the model of the Kingdoms of Consciousness, you'll be able to sail through the rest of the book and apply the core principles of the Anger Mastery Process.

Think of Chapter 3 as your intellectual "boot camp." The gym membership stretches, trains and strengthens your body. Chapter 3 will stretch, train and strengthen your mind.

# Chapter 3
# Victim Consciousness

It's time for another wake-up call. You spend most of your life living as a victim. Anytime you're angry or afraid, you experience your reality from Victim Consciousness.

Before we go any further, I'd like to address any judgments coming up for you around being called a victim or the fact that you spend most of your life living in Victim Consciousness. First of all, more than 85% of the world lives in Victim Consciousness full time (more than 55% of the United States). The rest of us have vacation homes there. There's nothing wrong with choosing to live in Victim Consciousness, but chances are that you live there only because you don't know how to leave. In the next few chapters you'll learn how to leave Victim Consciousness, and you'll also discover what drew you there in the first place. But in order for any of that information to make sense to you, first you have to learn what Victim Consciousness is.

Rev. Dr. Michael Beckwith (whom you might know from *The Secret*) popularized a model of consciousness developed by his mentor, the late Dr. Homer Johnson. This model divides human consciousness into four "kingdoms." Each Kingdom of Consciousness represents a different and unique experience of reality.

**First Kingdom** is **Victim Consciousness,** and it's where you, and most of the rest of the world, spend most of your time. When you're in First Kingdom, things are done *to* you.

**Second Kingdom** is where you begin to take back your power and manifest things using reason, logic and the linear mind. In Second Kingdom, things are done *by* you.

**Third Kingdom** represents higher spiritual states. They are nonlinear, and beyond both the world of form and the Law of Cause and Effect. In Third Kingdom, things are done *through* you.

**Fourth Kingdom** contains the realms of consciousness known as enlightenment. Beckwith says in Fourth Kingdom, things are done *as* you.[1]

At any given moment, your experience of the world—and more importantly, how happy you are with it—depends on which Kingdom of Consciousness you're in. Think about a time when you were depressed, and remember how the world looked to you then. Now, think about a time when you were in love, and remember how the world looked.

The world didn't just *look* different based on how you were feeling; the world actually *was* different. To understand why this is true, we need to explore the nature of reality itself.

## The Nature of Reality

Okay, you've arrived at the biggest, most challenging concept in this entire book. Understanding this concept is the key to becoming truly, incredibly happy. But *really* understanding it takes time and patience.

---

[1] I disagree with this, because when you reach the levels of consciousness of Fourth Kingdom, there is no longer a *you* for things to be done *as*.

What makes understanding this concept so challenging is that I can't prove it to you. It's not something that can be backed up with science (although the cutting edge of quantum physics is getting pretty close). This is a Big Truth, and that means it's *confirmable*, but not *provable*. It's something you'll have to explore yourself and discover how true it is for you.

To begin with, I'd like you to consider that there are two different kinds of reality: the "Big R" Reality and the "little r" reality.[2] The "Big R" Reality is infinite. It contains everything in the world. Your "little r" reality is finite. It contains everything in *your* world. Your "little r" reality is a very small part of the "Big R" Reality.

Think of it this way: the "Big R" Reality contains everything. *Everything* includes experiences like poverty, war and oppression. I accept that these things exist in the world; however, they don't exist in *my* world. I don't have any personal experience of them. They're not a part of my "little r" reality, and they're probably not a part of your "little r" reality, either.

Are you with me so far?

Because your "little r" reality contains only the things that you personally experience, what you experience as real is determined by where you put your attention. If you don't notice something, you don't experience it, so it's not real to you. What you *do* notice fills your entire reality.

You're a lot like a radio. No matter how many different stations are broadcasting, a radio can tune to only one frequency at a time, and that frequency determines what kind of music it

---

[2] Some people have suggested that "reality television" should be included as a third type of reality. This is silly because "reality television" does not, in fact, depict anyone's experience of reality. One of the *Real Housewives* claims to have a pet unicorn.

will play. If you pick a rock station, your "little r" reality will be filled with rock music. As long as you stay tuned to that frequency, you'll never hear any classical music.

How happy you are with this depends on whether or not you enjoy rock music. If you like rock music, you'll be happy. If you don't like rock music, and would prefer to listen to classical music, you won't be happy.

Right now, all you can do is listen to the rock music and get angry that the rock music station doesn't play the classical music you want to hear. But the Anger Mastery Process gives you another option. It lets you choose to tune to a different frequency so that your "little r" reality is filled with the kind of music you enjoy.

Ready for the next bit?

Consider the chair (or sofa, or bed) you're sitting on now. It's completely real to you. It's solid, and it's supporting your weight. You can see and feel it. You can hear it. You can smell it. You can even taste it, if you're into that sort of thing. But the truth is that there's almost nothing there but empty space. If you looked at that chair through an electron microscope, you'd realize that it's just a lot of molecules floating around, not touching each other. There's no reason why you shouldn't fall through the chair.

The reason you don't fall on the floor (or *through* the floor, because the floor's just a lot of empty space, too) is that you *tell yourself* that the chair and the floor are solid. In fact, the reason that you believe that you can see, feel, hear, smell and/or taste the chair is that you *tell yourself* you can. There is a voice in your head that narrates and describes every single experience to you, and that's what makes the experience real.

The fact is that you know something is real because you *tell yourself* it is. Everything you experience in your "little r" reality is a story. It's all made up of words.

Still with me? Good. This next part may be a bit of a stretch. You may want to sit down.[3]

Just because something is *real*, doesn't mean it's *true*.

Your "little r" reality is *subjective*. No matter what you experience, it always feels equally as real. When you dream, it feels completely real. When you wake up, *that's* completely real, too. You can't compare two experiences and say that one was more real than the other.

*Truth*, on the other hand, is *objective*. You can compare two experiences (both of which feel equally as real), and see that one is more *true* than the other.

Each time you take a step back and see the bigger picture, you expand the context of your story. Remember, the "Big R" Reality includes *everything*. When you expand the context of your story, you make your "little r" reality bigger. The more your "little r" reality includes, the more closely it resembles the "Big R" Reality, and the more true it is.

## The Science of Truth

Dr. David R. Hawkins is the foremost researcher in the field of human consciousness. All of Dr. Hawkins' research is based on the science of applied kinesiology, also known as muscle testing. It's been extensively documented that the body's acupuncture system has the ability to tell if something is beneficial or harmful

---

[3] That is, if you still believe that there's anything there for you to sit down on. Or with, for that matter.

to the body. When in the presence of something that supports the body, the acupuncture system gives a positive response, and the muscle being tested is strong. When in the presence of something that is harmful to the body, the acupuncture system gives a non-response, and the muscles go weak.

The breakthrough which formed the basis of Dr. Hawkins' research was the discovery that muscle testing can be used definitively to tell the difference between truth and falsehood in any context or situation. The acupuncture system of the body gives a strong response in the presence of truth, but does not respond in the presence of falsehood.

All of Dr. Hawkins' findings have been documented and repeated hundreds of thousands of times, in multiple situations and contexts. The results are consistent both when testing the arm strength of a naïve subject and when measuring an involuntary reaction in the human eye (the pupil dilates for a fraction of a second in the presence of falsehood). You can learn more about Dr. Hawkins' work in the Appendix. For now, it may be enough for you to accept that what I'm presenting to you is the result of more than 20 years of cutting-edge scientific research.

Using applied kinesiology, Dr. Hawkins developed a Map of Human Consciousness. This map includes the full range of "little r" realities that can be experienced by humans. The calibrations on the scale of consciousness go from 1 (the lowest amount of energy needed for something to be alive) to 1,000 (the highest possible consciousness that can be experienced in human form; this is the level of consciousness of Christ, Krishna, and Buddha, and only a few individuals in the history of the world have attained it). The scale is logarithmic, which means that each time it moves up a point, it's actually a factor of 10. In other words, it's not 1, 2, 3, 4, 5..., it's 1, 10, 100, 1,000, 10,000, 100,000, etc. Even a one-point increase represents a massive increase in energy.

I've taken this map and combined it with the model of the Four Kingdoms of Consciousness, as you can see in Figure 1.

Each point on the map represents its own "little r" reality, defined by the amount of available energy. Dr. Hawkins also determined the emotions and feelings that are the most dominant at the different levels of consciousness. You'll notice that the less energy available, the less attractive those "little r" realities are.

What Dr. Hawkins discovered is that the critical point on the scale is at calibration level 200. Anything that calibrates below 200 causes the acupuncture system to go weak. Anything that calibrates above 200 causes the acupuncture system to go strong. Notice that everything which calibrates below 200 falls within First Kingdom or Victim Consciousness. In Victim Consciousness, you encounter Pride, Anger, Desire, Fear, Grief, Apathy, Guilt and Shame, which coincidentally is also the name of the worst law firm *ever*.

Everything that calibrates below 200 represents **force**, while everything that calibrates above 200 represents increasing levels of **power**. Understanding the difference between power and force is one of the keys to getting happy.

**Force** is inherently weak. Force does not have enough energy to sustain itself, so it consumes energy. Force is always looking outside of itself for survival. Force moves in a negative (downward) direction. It is destructive, and does not support life. Force always

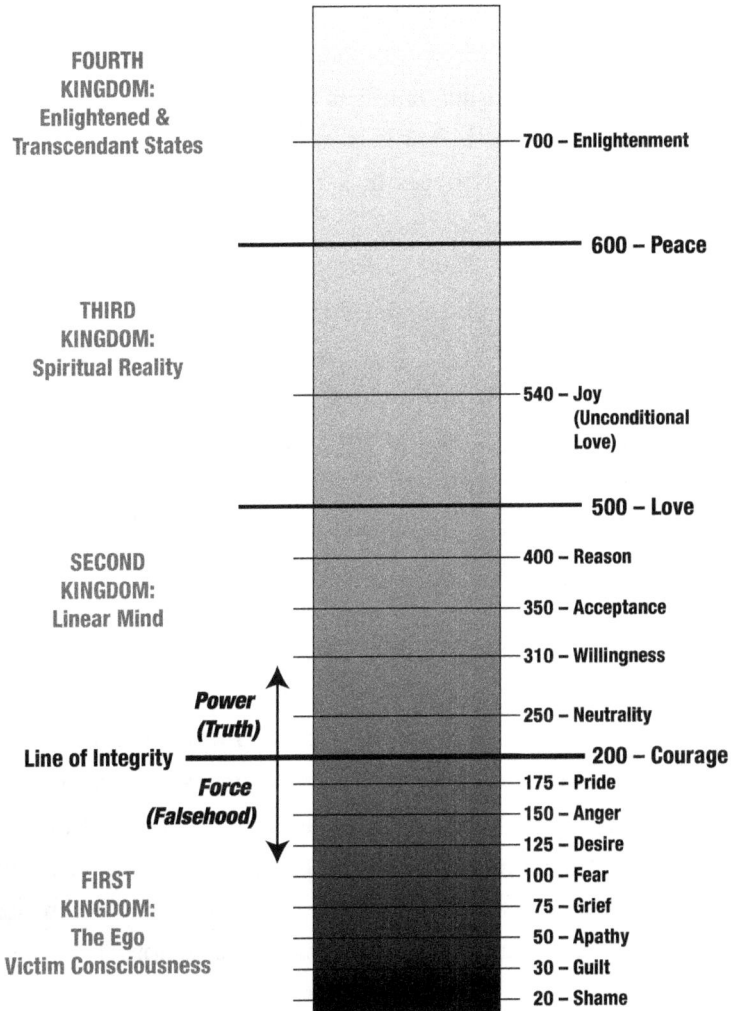

FOURTH KINGDOM:
Enlightened &
Transcendant States

700 – Enlightenment

600 – Peace

THIRD KINGDOM:
Spiritual Reality

540 – Joy
(Unconditional Love)

500 – Love

SECOND KINGDOM:
Linear Mind

400 – Reason

350 – Acceptance

310 – Willingness

*Power (Truth)*

250 – Neutrality

Line of Integrity — 200 – Courage

*Force (Falsehood)*

175 – Pride

150 – Anger

125 – Desire

FIRST KINGDOM:
The Ego
Victim Consciousness

100 – Fear

75 – Grief

50 – Apathy

30 – Guilt

20 – Shame

**Figure 1: Combined Map of Consciousness**

creates a counter-force; there is always something working against it. When you act from Anger, which calibrates at 150, you use force, which is why you're never happy with the outcome.

**Power**, on the other hand, is strong. Power has enough energy to sustain itself. Power is self-sufficient. Power, in fact, creates energy. Power moves in a positive (upward) direction. Power is creative, and nurtures and supports life. And there is no opposite to power. Power is free to grow and expand because there isn't anything working against it.

The way to become happy is to move upward on the map of consciousness. The more energy you have, the better you feel, and the happier you are. The single biggest boost to your happiness that you can experience comes from getting out of Victim Consciousness. Dr. Hawkins has calibrated the rate of happiness at each of the levels of consciousness. The level of Shame (20) has only a 1% rate of happiness; Guilt (30) has a 4% rate; Apathy (50) has a 5% rate; Grief (75) has a 9% rate; both Fear (100) and Desire (125) have a 10% rate; Anger (150) has a 12% rate; and Pride (175) has a 22% rate of happiness.[4] As soon as you step out of Victim Consciousness and move into integrity in Second Kingdom at the level of Courage (200), the rate of happiness more than doubles to 55%. When you begin to feel truly Safe (which you'll learn in Phase 2) and reach the level of Neutrality (250), the rate of happiness is 60%, five times greater than it is at the level of Anger.[5]

The map of consciousness is a valuable tool. Once you've identified where you are on the map based on how you're feeling,

---

[4] And a 78% chance of a fall.

[5] David R. Hawkins, M.D., Ph.D., *Transcending the Levels of Consciousness: The Stairway to Enlightenment* (Sedona, AZ: Veritas Publishing, 2006), 30.

you can easily choose the next better-feeling thought and move up the scale one level at a time.

Anger is a part of Victim Consciousness. This means it represents force, and is inherently negative. Even so, Anger doesn't always feel bad. Anger has more energy (and feels better) than Grief, Fear or Desire. If you're coming from one of those "little r" realities, Anger feels good. On the other hand, Anger has less energy than Pride, Courage or Neutrality, and so by comparison, Anger feels bad.

The real challenge with the linear model of the map is, it appears that when you advance up the scale, you escape the negative energies of Victim Consciousness. This is not accurate. When you step into integrity in Second Kingdom, you're no longer *limited* by the ego and the negativity of Victim Consciousness, but you can still experience those energies. A more accurate representation of the levels of consciousness might look like Figure 2. This model illustrates that each increased level of consciousness is an expanded context which includes all of the lower vibrations. It also better represents how even a slight increase in vibration results in a significant increase in power.

Everyone has a dominant vibration—a level of consciousness that defines most of his or her "little r" reality. However, you can operate from almost any place on the map, depending on what story you tell.

For example, say you're working hard to get a promotion at work. You're going to school and learning new skills, and this means you're operating from Second Kingdom, using your linear, rational mind.

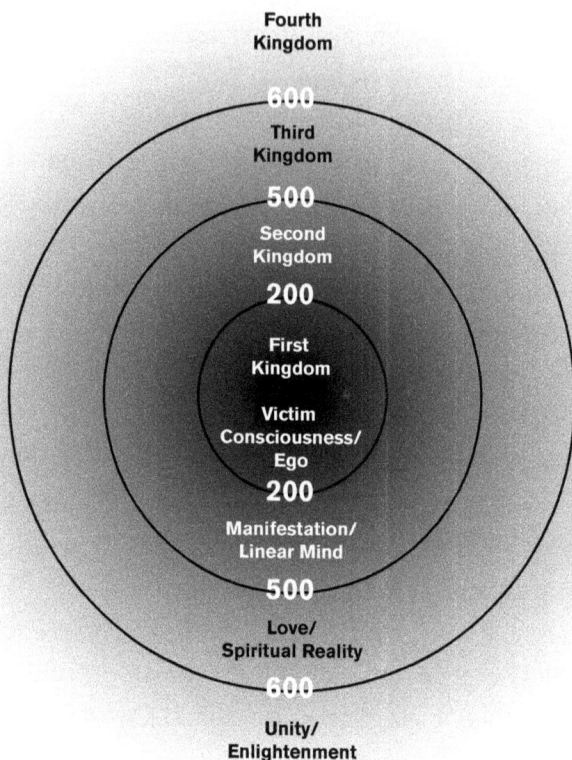

**Figure 2: Area Map of Consciousness**

When you meditate or experience spiritual community, your heart opens. You begin to feel connected to other people on a deeper and more profound level. This gives you a taste of the energy of Third Kingdom.

And for most of us, when the holidays roll around, we get together with our families right in the heart of First Kingdom.

# The Facts of Victim Consciousness

The most important fact to know about Victim Consciousness is that you won't find happiness there. If you care about being happy, the most effective way to do that is to get out of Victim Consciousness. In Chapter 4, I'll show you how. Chapter 5 will help you appreciate why you choose to spend time there in the first place. But right now, you need to understand how the "little r" realities of Victim Consciousness operate. Victim Consciousness can be a very grim place, so always remember, when you're in Victim Consciousness, everything you experience is *real*, but none of it is *true*.

## A Dog-Eat-Dog World

If you had to describe Victim Consciousness in just two words, they would be "not enough." In the "little r" realities of First Kingdom, there's a limited supply of everything. No matter what it is that you want, there's not enough of it to go around. This means that everyone competes with everyone else in order to survive.

Not only is the supply limited, but it's also fixed. When you operate from Victim Consciousness, you play a zero-sum game. In order for you to win, someone else has to lose, and the only way to get something is to take it away from someone else.

Money is usually the biggest motivator in Victim Consciousness. The more money you have, the less money other people have, and vice versa. The reason that you have so little money available to you now is because all of the money and resources in the world have been trickling upstream into the pockets of *The Rich*. If you don't believe me, ask yourself how much you paid for gas the last time you filled up your car's tank. *The Rich* thank you for your contribution.

Money isn't the only limited resource in Victim Consciousness. There's also not enough love, success or freedom. Not only do you have to fight to get enough resources just to survive (thriving is not a realistic option in Victim Consciousness), but once you get those resources, you have to fight to keep them.

There's no such thing as cooperation in Victim Consciousness. You can't trust anyone but yourself. Anyone who seems to want to help you is only looking for a way to take advantage of you. That's okay, though. You accept their help only because you hope you'll have the chance to take advantage of them first.

Everything in Victim Consciousness seems to be a win/lose scenario, but in fact, even this isn't even true. In Victim Consciousness, no one ever wins. Every scenario is lose/lose.

## Through the Looking Glass

When you step into Victim Consciousness, you go through the looking glass. Everything in Victim Consciousness is backwards. One of Dr. Hawkins' most significant discoveries is that in Victim Consciousness, even the energy system of your body is inverted. Instead of giving a strong response in the presence of truth, your acupuncture system gives a strong response in the *absence* of truth. This is why the muscle test can be used accurately only by about a third of the population of the United States.

When you operate from Victim Consciousness, the things you think will make you feel better will actually make you feel worse.

Most importantly, once you step into Victim Consciousness, it's almost impossible to find your way back out again. Each time you think you're heading out, you're actually heading deeper in. There is, however, a quick and easy way to jump out of Victim Consciousness and back into integrity, and you'll learn it in the next chapter.

## Every Action Is Counter-Productive

The last fact to know about Victim Consciousness is that when you're there, any action you take will be counter-productive. No matter what choice you make or what intention you set, it will be wrong. When you act from Victim Consciousness, you use force, not power. This means you will always create a counter-force. The harder you try, the more resistance you'll create. It is possible to get what you want, but it's never worth the effort, and it won't make you happy.

This is the reason that I urged you not to set any weight loss or fitness goals when you began Phase 1. The original intention behind those goals would have come from Victim Consciousness, and not only would you not succeed in making the changes to your physical body that you want, but you would eventually get discouraged and stop exercising. This would make it harder for you to move out of Victim Consciousness. When you get to Phase 3, you'll be able to set goals that support you.

# The Facts of Integrity

Once you step out of Victim Consciousness and into integrity in Second Kingdom, everything changes. The biggest change is that you experience sufficiency, and notice that you do, in fact, have enough of the things you need to survive. As you advance in consciousness, you encounter the truth of **Abundance**, and discover that there is no limit to the Good that you can enjoy.

When you operate from integrity, your "little r" reality represents increasing levels of truth. You soon discover that there is no competition. Your prosperity and success have no connection to anyone else's. Your Good is *your* Good. No one can take it from you, and you're not taking it from anyone else.

When you act from integrity, you use power, not force. Instead of conflict and resistance, you attract support and cooperation. Your intentions and goals almost always turn out better than you could imagine.

Most importantly, when you act from integrity, you get to be happy. The more time you spend in integrity, the happier you become.

Moving out of Victim Consciousness into integrity is very simple. All you have to do is answer one question: Whose business is it?

# Chapter 4
# Leaving Victim Consciousness: Whose Business Is It?

**B**yron Katie is an author and speaker who created a powerful process called "The Work." In her first book, *Loving What Is,* Katie suggests that there are three types of business in the world: "My Business," "Your Business" ("Other People's Business"), and "God's Business." She points out that anytime you find yourself in "Other People's Business" or "God's Business," you feel stressed. Why? Because you don't have any business in "Other People's Business" or "God's Business." When you're in "Other People's Business," or "God's Business," you have no control and no influence. In fact, when you're in "Other People's Business" or "God's Business," you are powerless.[1]

Put another way, when you're in "Other People's Business," or "God's Business," you're in Victim Consciousness, so any action you take will only make things worse.

**Just because you're involved in something doesn't make it your business.** You spend far less time in "My Business," than you might think. In fact, you probably spend most of your time

[1] Byron Katie, *Loving What Is: Four Questions that Can Change Your Life* (New York: Harmony Books, 2002), 3.

in "Other People's Business." This isn't necessarily a bad thing, as long as you can recognize when you're in "Other People's Business," and know how to step back into "My Business."

Because you spend so much of your life in "Other People's Business" and so little time in "My Business," you may need some help with telling them apart. To illustrate, I've created a few flow charts that will help you to become familiar with this process.

## Is the Government My Business?

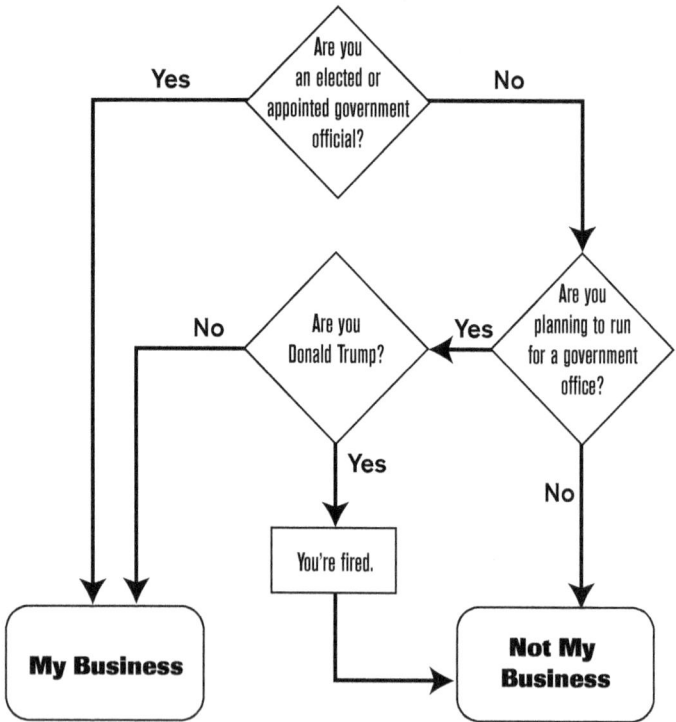

**Figure 3: Is the Government My Business?**

# Is the Conflict in the Middle East My Business?

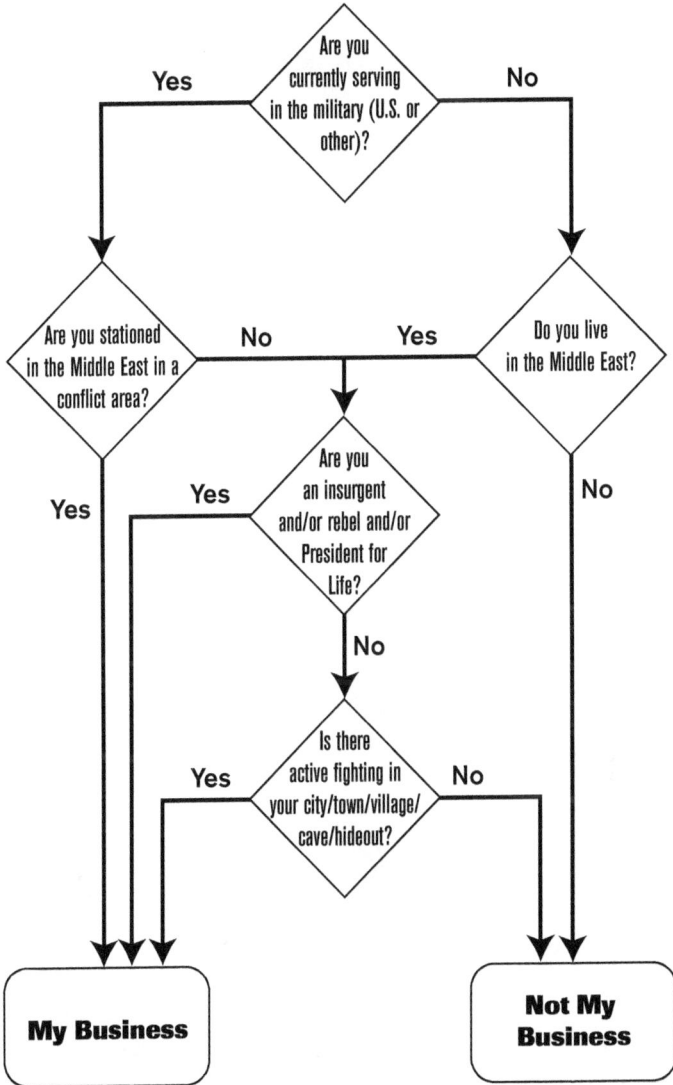

**Figure 4: Is the Conflict in the Middle East My Business?**

## Is the Economy My Business?

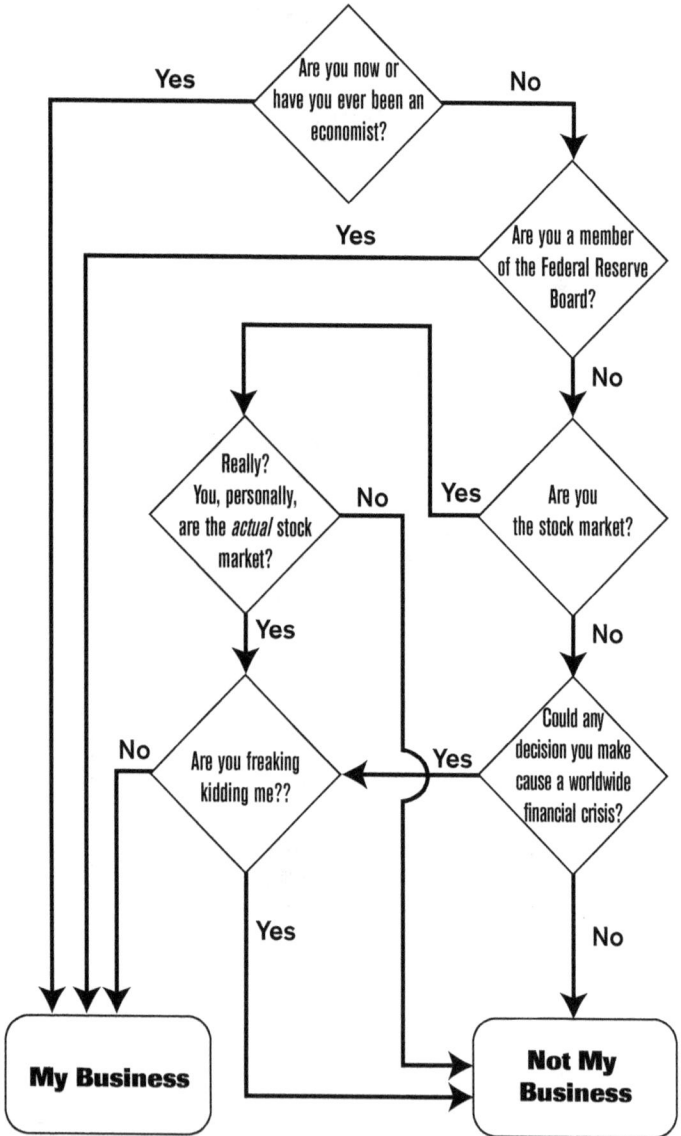

Figure 5: Is the Economy My Business?

"My Business," consists exclusively of things that directly affect you, which are actually your responsibility, and that you have the power and ability to influence or change. If it doesn't directly affect you, isn't your responsibility, and/or you can't do anything about it, it's not your business.

## Does It Affect You, Personally?

This is the most important question, and it's one that has to be applied with absolute precision. In order for something to be "My Business," it has to affect you, personally, *right now*. Just because something could, possibly, at some point in the future affect you doesn't make it your business. If and when it begins to actually affect you, it *might be* your business, as long as it's also your responsibility and you can do something about it. Until then, it's none of your business.

Even if something does affect you, personally right now, it doesn't have to be "My Business." Consider applying the "ignore it and see if it goes away" test. If you ignore a situation and it eventually goes away without causing you any harm, it's none of your business.

## Is It Really Your Responsibility?

Personally, I struggle with this one the most. My ego believes that it is my responsibility to make sure everyone I encounter follows the rules. If anyone breaks the rules, he or she must face the wrath of my ego. I've come to terms with the fact that my ego is a cross between Superman and Serpico. Smoke in a nonsmoking area, park in a random, illegal manner, or just walk into the sauna at the gym while wearing shoes (ignoring the sign that clearly states that shoes are not allowed in the sauna), and my ego jumps to attention. Rules are being broken and justice must be done!

There's only one catch: it's not my responsibility to dole out justice in these situations. I didn't make the rules. I don't even understand some of the rules. (Why can't you wear shoes in the sauna? Are they going to melt?) And when I see other people ignoring the rules, it truly pisses me off. What it doesn't do, however, is make it my responsibility. I'm not an officer of the law. I'm not even a mall cop. I don't work at the gym. What other people do, even when it's rude, inconsiderate, and in direct violation of the rules, is not my business, because enforcing the rules is not my responsibility.

You know what else isn't my responsibility? Other people's lives. It's not my responsibility to stop my friends or family from making what I know will be stupid, unfortunate, painful choices. It's not my responsibility to take care of anyone but myself. And it's not my responsibility to make anyone else happy.

And just in case I'm being too subtle here, it's not *your* responsibility, either.

There are, however, exceptions to this. For example, parents *are* responsible for their children, at least until those children are old enough to be responsible for themselves. Much of the time, it will be moot, though. In order for your children to be your business, they need to be your responsibility *and* you have to be able to influence their behavior. Good luck with that.

## Do I Have Any Power or Influence to Change It?

If you encounter a situation that affects you personally right now, and is actually your responsibility, the last thing you need to ask is if you have any power or influence over the situation. Are you able to change, adjust, modify or alter the circumstances in any way? If changing, adjusting, modifying or altering the circumstances requires that you get other people to change *their* behavior, then the answer is no. There's nothing you can do to get anyone else to behave the way you would like them to behave.[2]

If you can accept that you have no power to change anyone else's behavior, you'll save yourself a tremendous amount of suffering, and significantly cut down on the amount of time you spend in Victim Consciousness. Once you move out of Victim Consciousness, you'll discover that there are other options. Instead of using force to try to control others, which creates a lose/lose scenario, you can use power to create a win/ win scenario, in which everyone is happy. But you can do that only from within "My Business."

# The Appeal of "Other People's Business"

Because you spend so much of your time in "Other People's Business," it's reasonable to wonder what the appeal is. You mainly go to "Other People's Business," in order to feel Anger and Pride. When you're in "Other People's Business," you can get involved in other people's conflicts, challenges and fights, and no matter the outcome, it won't affect you, personally, because it's none of your business. You also get to judge others and feel smugly superior to them. Come to think of it, you spend time in "Other People's Business" for the same reasons people watch reality television.

---

[2] If you don't believe me, ask my father.

Anger and Pride are both part of Victim Consciousness, so they're fundamentally negative, painful feelings. However, they feel good by comparison with Desire, Fear, Apathy, Grief, Guilt and Shame. When you step into "Other People's Business," you get to experience pure Anger and Pride, without feeling any of the Guilt, Grief, Fear and Shame you have to acknowledge when you're in "My Business."

This is only a short-term solution to your pain, however. Any action you take from these levels of consciousness will be counter-productive and make you feel worse, dragging you deeper into Victim Consciousness. The only way to make the good feelings last is to use the Anger as a springboard to jump into integrity in Second Kingdom and back into "My Business."

## Practical Applications of "Whose Business Is It?"

For many years, I suffered from noisy neighbors. Since I rarely watched the news, my noisy neighbors were my main source of anger. I lived in one apartment for over 14 years, and having to complain to the landlord (and, on multiple occasions, the police) to get some peace and quiet was a regular part of my "little r" reality. Eventually, I moved to a new, nicer apartment. There were only four units in my building, and my neighbors were quiet. Unfortunately, the neighbors in the other buildings had a gaggle of free-range children who ran wild and made huge amounts of noise.

I, of course, was absolutely within my rights to complain. My lease agreement explicitly guaranteed my right to quiet enjoyment. The lease also forbade socializing in the common areas or playing in the parking lots. What I could never do was get the management to enforce the lease.

I complained—a lot—and I got angry. This did not improve the situation. One day I found myself standing on my balcony screaming at the kids—and at the adults responsible for them—that they were violating the lease and needed to shut the hell up.

That's when it hit me. I had let my anger take over, and turn me into a complete asshole. Who was that guy? That couldn't possibly be me! This was not even remotely spiritual behavior. I had, as they say, hit rock bottom.

I took a step back and decided to listen to some of my own advice. I was obviously *way* outside of the boundaries of "My Business." It's not my business to enforce the rules. It's not possible for me to change anyone else's behavior. And every time I told myself differently, I hopped on the express train to Victim Consciousness.

I had to accept the truth that my noisy neighbors and their free-range children are none of my business. Whenever I heard noise, I had a choice. I could choose to get angry, or I could choose to stay in "My Business," and focus on something else.

I resolved to walk my talk and stay in "My Business." This was not easy. I must have repeated "This is none of my business," more than fifty times a day that first week. The more I practiced it, though, the easier it got.

Then one day, a few weeks later, I realized that I didn't notice the noise anymore. I don't know if the noise just stopped bothering me, or if my neighbors decided to corral their kids. All I know is that one day I looked up and realized I hadn't been angry about the noise in weeks, and I also hadn't noticed the kids playing in my parking lot or around my building.

It didn't matter if I stopped noticing or if they stopped making noise. All that mattered was that because I chose to stay in "My Business," within a very short time, I became significantly happier.

# Acting In "My Business"

The situations that fall within "My Business," affect you personally, are your responsibility, and you have the ability to influence them. These situations can still make you angry, but because they're a part of "My Business," you can actually do something about them. So here's the most important (and difficult) advice I can give you: *Don't.*

Don't do anything to change or influence the situation, even though you technically could. It doesn't matter that the situation is a part of "My Business"; if you act from anger and direct it at the situation, you will be using force, not power. This means no matter what action you take, it will make things worse.

Take that excess energy and work it off at the gym. Use it to clean your garage, do your taxes or remodel your kitchen. Whatever you do, don't take any action to change the situation while you still feel any anger about it. In Phase 2, you'll learn a technique that will speed up this process and let you respond using power, rather than react using force. *Then*, you can address the situation itself.

There's more to Victim Consciousness than just "Other People's Business," and before you can move out, you need to become aware of why you moved in. First Kingdom has a hell of a sales pitch … but you have to watch out for the fine print.

# Chapter 5
# The Lure of Victim Consciousness

**N**ow that you know how to get out of Victim Consciousness, let's explore why you would want to go there in the first place.

The appeal of Victim Consciousness is all in the marketing. First of all, they never call it Victim Consciousness; they call it First Kingdom, which tested much better in the focus groups. It sounds exclusive and lavish, and it's first, so it must be the best.

It's no wonder that the sales pitch for Victim Consciousness is so compelling: Desire lives in the heart of First Kingdom. The ads and billboards and commercials all promise such wonderful experiences, and in such big, easy-to-read print. You find yourself wanting these experiences so badly that you don't bother to read the fine print. But beware: the big print giveth, but the fine print taketh away. Consider this chapter to be a magnifying glass. It's time for you to read the fine print.

## The Sales Pitch: No Pressure, No Responsibility, and No Blame

Are you carrying the weight of the world on your shoulders? Is your life filled with obligations and duties that you'd rather avoid? Does it seem like no matter how often you eat all of your vegetables, you never get dessert?

Well, take a vacation from all of the pressure and responsibility of your life and spend some time in First Kingdom! Leave your cares and obligations at the door. When you come to First Kingdom, your life is no longer your problem. You don't have to worry about deadlines or promises, or obligations. In First Kingdom, you get to focus on you.

You know what else you don't have to worry about in First Kingdom? Consequences! If things start to fall apart (and rest assured, they will), it won't be your fault. How could it be your fault? It wasn't your responsibility! Sure, there will be a lot of finger-pointing and trying to place the blame, but none of the blame will ever stick to you. Because nothing is your fault, you can't be punished or held accountable.

Isn't it time to let someone else do the work and be responsible? Aren't you entitled to a break? Come back to First Kingdom! We're waiting for you!

## The Fine Print

When you give up responsibility, you must also give up your power.

The reason that nothing is ever your fault is that no matter the situation, you are the victim: impotent, marginalized, abused and weak. No one expects you to succeed at anything.

When you give up your power, responsibility, and accountability, you forfeit your ability to express yourself creatively.

When you give up the risk, you also give up the reward. Being immune to blame means you are ineligible to receive credit, validation, or appreciation.

# The Sales Pitch:
# You're Entitled to Special Treatment

Don't you hate it when other people are the center of attention? All of a sudden, *their* needs are more important than yours are. What about *your* needs? What about *you*?

Well, when you step into First Kingdom, it's *all* about you. When you're in First Kingdom, you are the center of the universe. No matter what you want, what you need, or what you feel, it's automatically more important than anyone else's wants, needs, or feelings. Why? Because it's *you*!

In First Kingdom you're free from those annoying rules and social conventions that apply to other people. Other people have to RSVP to an invitation and show up on time, but not you. You can show up whenever you want—or even decide at the last minute not to go at all because you're not feeling up to it. It's okay! You're entitled to put yourself first. The best part is that people can't get angry or upset about how your behavior affected them, because you're more important than they are. They actually have to feel concern and sympathy for you.

And no matter where you go, you get to arrange everything so that it works for you. People will have to go out of their way to accommodate your every whim, and they can't complain about it. Plus, you never have to do anything for yourself, because you can always get other people to do it for you. It's like being royalty!

## The Fine Print

Special treatment and entitlements are based on the degree of physical, mental, emotional and/or psychological suffering you experience. Full entitlements do not take effect until you have attained formal recognition as being "disabled" or "handicapped." (See disclaimer below.)

The value and convenience of the entitlements you may receive will never exceed the cost in terms of personal discomfort, limitation, pain, and suffering.

While others will be obliged to do things for you, you will rarely, if ever, be satisfied with the results. You are entitled to complain about the results; however, there is a limit to how many times you can compel other people to make alterations or changes before they become entitled to abandon you. Be aware that once you ask someone to do something for you, you are no longer allowed to do it for yourself. Doing it for yourself (to get it right) will immediately revoke any and all entitlements of First Kingdom.

**Important Disclaimer:** Note that being recognized as "disabled" or "handicapped" does not automatically mean that you are subject to the reality of First Kingdom. Physical, mental, emotional, and/or psychological challenges are insufficient on their own. To be eligible for the entitlements of First Kingdom, you must also embrace your identity as a victim, wallow in self-pity, and demand sympathy, attention, and special treatment from others. Self-responsibility, personal accountability, integrity, and/or a positive attitude will automatically exclude you from any of the entitlements offered in Victim Consciousness.

# The Sales Pitch: You Get to Be Right and Prove that Others are Wrong

Are there four more satisfying words in the English language than "I told you so"? It's almost impossible to say them without doing a little dance. Sure, when you say them, you may have to look all crushed and sympathetic on the outside, but on the inside, you're doing the "I Was Right Rhumba."[1]

Well, here in First Kingdom, our motto is, "If you love to be right, we're the right place for you." We specialize in all forms of vindication. Have you been mistreated, injured, overlooked, discriminated against, spurned, or simply ignored? We have attorneys on call 24 hours a day, waiting to turn your bruised ego into cold, hard cash. It doesn't matter if your spouse left you for a younger model, if you got passed over for a promotion, or if your morning coffee was just too darned hot. Attention must be paid!

Of course, here in First Kingdom, we understand that it's not always about the money. Sometimes, it's the principle that counts. Did your parents not support your dreams? Were you a constant disappointment to them? What about high school? Were you bullied and ridiculed? Humiliated at the prom by your secret crush? In First Kingdom, we believe that living well is the best revenge. We'll help you to create a life specifically designed to embarrass and humble everyone who ever disrespected you. If you're willing to put in some effort, you can become the envy of everyone you've ever known. You can have it all—money, power, and fame—and best of all, you can rub their noses in your success. Who has the power now? You do! And you get to lord it over them for the rest of your life.

---

[1] Other dances include the "Told You So Tango," the "Suck it Samba," the "In Your Face Fandango," and the "Booya Boogie." The "Ha Ha Horah" is usually reserved for weddings and Bar Mitzvahs.

## The Fine Print

Being right and/or proving that you were right in no way guarantees that you will also be happy. The process of proving that you were right requires a tremendous amount of energy, and employs force. This means it will be a constant struggle, with obstacles and opposition at every turn.

No matter how often you are right and prove other people wrong, they will never appreciate you for it. It doesn't matter if you demonstrate beyond any doubt that you, in fact, did know what was best for them, they will be ungrateful and resent you.

While it is possible to create a life that elicits feelings of envy, pride, desire, and/or regret from others, the time and effort required to create this life far exceeds the duration of the pleasure you might experience from the reactions at a high-school reunion or family event. The chances that living this life will make you happy are slim.

Demonstrating how wrong others were for treating you poorly in the past does not guarantee that they will be inclined to treat you any better in the future. This is particularly true when you argue your case using attorneys and the legal system.

While it is true that in every legal action there are winners and there are losers, most of the time, the winners are the attorneys.

# The Sales Pitch: You Can Get What You Want If You Work Hard Enough

Whatever you conceive, you can achieve! That's not just the American Dream, that's the promise that awaits you in First Kingdom. You can have everything you ever wanted, as long as you want it badly enough. Let's face it, it's a competitive world. Are you willing to do whatever it takes to get what you want? Are you willing to keep your eye on the prize and not let yourself be distracted by anyone or anything? Then First Kingdom is the right place for you! In First Kingdom, as long as you're focused, determined, and ruthless enough, eventually you can force your dreams to come true. If you're ready to accept that the end always justifies the means, you could be the next big success story in First Kingdom.

## The Fine Print

Getting what you want in no way guarantees that you'll be happy.

The effort and energy required to force your dreams to come true may exceed any value, pleasure, or happiness contained in those dreams.

When you get what you want, you won't be able to enjoy it. You'll be so drained from the struggle to get what you wanted that when you get it, you no longer want it as much. Once you have it, you will have to struggle to protect it so that it doesn't get taken away from you.

It is rarely possible to get what you want and maintain personal relationships. Your personal relationships may be damaged by your use of force, including Anger, Desire and Pride, in the pursuit of your goal.

Wanting is extremely addictive. The satisfaction you feel when you get what you want fades quickly, leaving you feeling empty. The only way to fill the void is to want (and get) more. The more you want, and the more you get, the less satisfied (and the less happy) you are.

Because First Kingdom is a zero-sum reality, in order to get what you want, you have to take it from someone else. This brings up unconscious Guilt, which makes you vulnerable to accident, loss, retribution and punishment. The more you get, the more Guilt you feel, and the less happy you will be. The only way that you will be able to purge this Guilt is by losing everything you have gained, accepting the Shame and humiliation as just punishment.

# How to Stop Them From Pulling You Back In

Victim Consciousness is a lot like the Mafia: every time you think you're out, it pulls you back in. The work you've been doing in Phase 1 helps you to get out of Victim Consciousness. In Phase 2, you'll learn how to *stay* out. And you'll do that by learning how to feel Safe.

# ANGER MASTERY

## PHASE 2

# Chapter 6
# Safety

**P**hase 2 of the Anger Mastery Process is all about Safety: how to recognize when you're not feeling Safe, and what do to in order to feel Safe. Even though Safety is one of the fundamental human needs, few people know how true Safety feels. To understand the importance of meeting your Safety Needs, we need to take a look at the concept of needs in general.

## Meet Your Needs[1]

Our story begins in a time of economic strife, political uncertainty, record unemployment, and global unrest—and no, I'm not talking about 2011. *This* story begins in the 1920s, the *first* time Wall Street's unregulated behavior plunged America into a Great Depression. A psychologist by the name of Abraham Maslow was preparing to revolutionize the entire field of head shrinking (which, at the time, had been around for about 30 years). Up until this point, psychology assumed that people were basically screwed up. The main objectives of psychology were to (a) figure out exactly how people were screwed up, (b) figure out how to blame it all on the patient's

---

[1] My editor complained about this heading because this section does not, in fact, tell you how to meet your needs. I said that if that's what I intended to do, I would have titled it "*How to* Meet Your Needs." In this section, you meet, or make the acquaintance of, your needs. I met her suggestion that I change the title to "Hello, Needs!" with thinly veiled contempt.

mother, and (c) figure out how to get patients to pay for a full hour, but only get 50 minutes.

Maslow approached things from the opposite direction. He wondered what would happen if instead of assuming people were fundamentally sick, we assumed people were fundamentally healthy. What motivates the behavior of healthy people? And more importantly, how do you get healthy people to pay for a full hour but give them only 50 minutes?

Maslow proposed that we are motivated by our unmet needs. He discovered that all needs are not created equal—some needs are more important than others. In fact, until we've met all of our "lower" needs, we won't be motivated to meet any of our "higher" needs. Maslow summed up his approach in a hierarchy of needs that's usually illustrated in a pyramid, as shown in Figure 6.

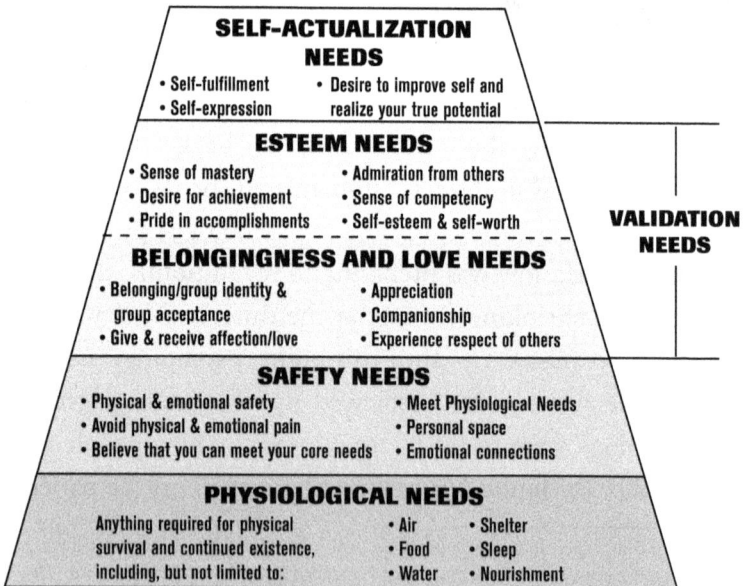

**SELF-ACTUALIZATION NEEDS**
- Self-fulfillment
- Self-expression
- Desire to improve self and realize your true potential

**ESTEEM NEEDS**
- Sense of mastery
- Desire for achievement
- Pride in accomplishments
- Admiration from others
- Sense of competency
- Self-esteem & self-worth

**BELONGINGNESS AND LOVE NEEDS**
- Belonging/group identity & group acceptance
- Give & receive affection/love
- Appreciation
- Companionship
- Experience respect of others

**SAFETY NEEDS**
- Physical & emotional safety
- Avoid physical & emotional pain
- Believe that you can meet your core needs
- Meet Physiological Needs
- Personal space
- Emotional connections

**PHYSIOLOGICAL NEEDS**
Anything required for physical survival and continued existence, including, but not limited to:
- Air
- Food
- Water
- Shelter
- Sleep
- Nourishment

**VALIDATION NEEDS**

**Figure 6: Maslow's Hierarchy of Needs**

## Physiological Needs

Your Physiological Needs include everything you need to survive, such as air, food, water, sleep, and shelter. You will do anything to meet these needs, and I do mean *anything*. If these needs aren't being met, the body's instinctive, animal nature takes over. It's not pretty.

## Safety Needs

Your Safety Needs include everything you *think* you need to survive. In fact, you *could* survive without most of these things, although probably not without whining about it. In order for you to meet your Safety Needs, you have to believe that your Physiological Needs will be met in the future. Your Safety Needs are what motivate you to avoid physical and emotional pain.

## Belongingness and Love Needs/ Esteem Needs

Maslow's next two categories have to do with being loved and appreciated in relationships. Belongingness and Love Needs are about being loved and appreciated by other people, and Esteem Needs are about being loved and appreciated by yourself. Since they're essentially the same thing, I've combined them into a single category called Validation Needs.

## Self-Actualization Needs

The highest needs in Maslow's pyramid are the Self-Actualization Needs. These are the things that you do to fulfill your potential as an individual.

# Need Bank Accounts

In my book, *The Relationship Handbook: How to Understand and Improve Every Relationship in Your Life,* I introduced a more dynamic model to understand our needs. Rather than working with Maslow's pyramid, I suggest a series of four Need Bank Accounts. I combined the Belongingness and Love Needs and Esteem Needs to form Validation Needs, as shown in Figure 7.

It's important to understand the relationship between your *wants* and your *needs*. As Maslow discovered, you're motivated by your *needs*, not by your *wants*. The reason that you want anything is that you believe that when you get the thing that you want, it will make a deposit in one or more of your Need Bank Accounts.

Each of your Need Bank Accounts has a minimum required balance, and you are responsible for maintaining that balance at all times. When you maintain the balance in a Need Bank Account, you experience that need as being met. Although you're motivated to maintain the minimum balance in *all* of your Need Bank Accounts, you always focus on meeting your

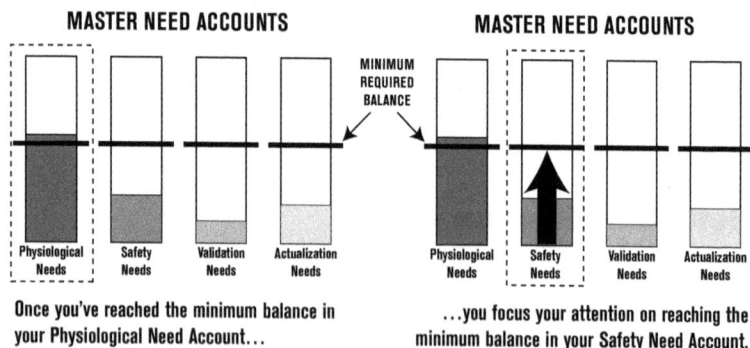

**MASTER NEED ACCOUNTS**

MINIMUM REQUIRED BALANCE

Physiological Needs | Safety Needs | Validation Needs | Actualization Needs

Once you've reached the minimum balance in your Physiological Need Account...

**MASTER NEED ACCOUNTS**

Physiological Needs | Safety Needs | Validation Needs | Actualization Needs

...you focus your attention on reaching the minimum balance in your Safety Need Account.

**Figure 7: Need Bank Accounts**

lower needs first. This model shows you what Maslow's pyramid doesn't, that each of your Need Bank Accounts is independent of the others. If the balance in your Safety Need Account is below the minimum level, you can still receive deposits in your Validation Need Account and your Self-Actualization Need Account. However, you won't *notice* those deposits until you've met your Safety Needs.

Now, you might look at this model, or at Maslow's pyramid, and assume that your Physiological Needs are the most important and, except in the most literal sense, you'd be wrong. Yes, you do need air, food, and water to survive, but for the most part, you don't worry about finding enough of these. Your Physiological Needs take care of themselves.

You might then assume that the most important needs are your Self-Actualization Needs because they're the highest needs, and represent how you live up to your ultimate potential, and you'd be batting a thousand in the World Series of Wrong. Most people never get close to experiencing a Self-Actualization Need. (Hint: Self-Actualization Needs *never* involve a featured role on a reality television show.)

So, now you might assume that since you've already eliminated half of the choices, you've got a pretty good chance of picking the right answer. Do yourself a favor and stop assuming. You're embarrassing yourself. If you already knew the answers, your name would be on the cover of this book instead of mine.

The most important needs are your Safety Needs. Once you learn how to maintain the minimum balance in your Safety Need Account, you'll easily and automatically meet all of your other needs.

# The Power of Pain

As soon as the balance in your Safety Need Account drops below the minimum level, you dive into Victim Consciousness. You'll stay in Victim Consciousness until you're able to meet your Safety Needs. While you're in Victim Consciousness, every action you take is motivated by your need for Safety. You want the things that you want because you believe getting those things will make deposits in your Safety Need Account and allow you to get out of Victim Consciousness. Unfortunately, when you act from Victim Consciousness, you use force instead of power. This means that every action that you take is counter-productive. The more you do, the less Safe you feel.

You know from the work you did in Phase 1 that when you're in Victim Consciousness, the solution is not to take any action until you're certain you've moved out of "Other People's Business," or "God's Business" and back into "My Business." This is not always easy to do, however, because when you step into Victim Consciousness, you experience pain. The pain might be physical pain, or it might be emotional pain. The type of pain doesn't matter. When you're in pain and you feel unsafe, you don't have the ability to identify what kind of pain it is. You also don't have the ability to ask whose business it is. All that matters is that you find a way to stop hurting. Pain is a very powerful motivator. The more pain you experience, the more you're willing to do to stop it, whatever the cost.

Let's say that you suffered from headaches—not your average tension or sinus headache, but blinding, throbbing, debilitating pain. What if I told you I had a solution? What if I had a device that would absolutely guarantee to stop the pain of a headache instantly? And more than that, what if once you used it, you would never, ever have another headache again? Now, this device isn't FDA approved (it's French), and it does have a few side effects, but would you be willing to risk them if it meant that you would never have to suffer one of those headaches ever again? Sure you would!

You may have heard of this device. It's been around since the eighteenth century. It's called a guillotine.

So, are you ready to give it a try? Of course not. The idea of chopping off your head so that you never have to experience another headache is insane. You would never, ever, consider it.

But here's the thing—you would never, ever consider it *now*, because now, you don't have a headache. But the next time you experience that blinding pain that fills your "little r" reality with endless agony, the guillotine may look more attractive. When you're in that much pain, you'll consider *anything* to stop it, even chopping off your own head. It doesn't matter that in the long term, chopping off your head would be counter-productive. All that matters is that it would stop the pain right now.

Emotional pain is just as powerful as physical pain. I point this out because you're living in a world of emotional pain. You may not notice it anymore because you've gotten very good at stuffing it, numbing it, and otherwise distracting yourself so you don't have to feel it, but it's still there. One of the ways that you avoid feeling this pain is by getting angry. When you get angry, you feel more powerful. Anger has more energy than the lower levels of consciousness of Fear, Grief, Guilt, and Shame that are the cause of your emotional pain, and so when you get Angry, you feel better.

However, Anger feels better only by comparison to the more painful feelings; it's still a part of Victim Consciousness. When you get angry, it doesn't mean that you've healed the pain; it just means that now you have enough energy to go out and find yourself a guillotine.

# The Panic Button: Fight or Flight

The moment the balance in your Safety Need Account drops below the minimum level and you step into Victim Consciousness, your ego pushes the Panic Button. The Panic Button triggers your sympathetic nervous system and initiates the "fight-or-flight" response. Adrenalin begins to course through your bloodstream, giving you extra energy, strength and focus. This is what enables a mother to single-handedly lift a Volkswagen to rescue her child. Your senses are heightened (as are your responses), and every nonessential bodily function is put on hold, giving you the ability either to defend yourself (fight) or run like hell (flight).

This is a biological survival response, and it's intended for emergencies only. You could call it your body's own 9-1-1 operator. The only difference is that when you dial 9-1-1 in the real world, you get a recording that tells you to make sure it's an actual emergency before you get help. Your internal 9-1-1 system doesn't have this feature. This means that every time the balance in your Safety Need Account drops below the minimum level, you go into fight-or-flight mode.

You might not think this is such a bad thing (and your ego certainly agrees with you). After all, if you don't feel Safe, you might assume that the burst of adrenaline, the extra energy and the heightened senses should make you feel a lot better.

This assumption isn't just wrong; it's wrong on multiple levels.

First, when you're in fight-or-flight, you're in Victim Consciousness, so any action you take uses *force* not *power*. This means that no matter what you do, it will ultimately be counter-productive. You think you're making yourself feel more Safe—and in the short term, it may work. But in the long term, you will feel even less Safe than you did when you started.

Second, the enhanced abilities you get from the fight-or-flight response are useful only in *actual* life-or-death situations. Getting selected for an IRS audit will drain your Safety Need Account (and probably your checking account as well), but the ability to lift a Volkswagen won't help you. Sure, it's impressive, but it's not tax deductible.

Third, as with all emergency services, the fight-or-flight response comes with a very big price tag. It's intended to be a last-ditch survival mechanism, used only in the most extreme conditions. Once you've either defeated the threat or escaped, you're supposed to go back to your cave and recover. The fight-or-flight response is like a cash advance on a biological credit card. Not only are there exorbitant up-front fees for the convenience, but you also pay the highest possible interest rate on the loan. If you're stranded in the middle of nowhere, it might be worth it, but you wouldn't want to use it to buy groceries.

You spend most of your life in Victim Consciousness, feeling unsafe, and locked in a perpetual state of fight-or-flight. You call this stress.

Anytime you feel stressed, you're unsafe. The balance in your Safety Need Account has dropped below the minimum level, you've stepped into Victim Consciousness, and your ego has pushed the Panic Button and dialed 9-1-1. The longer you feel stressed, the more likely it is that when your ego dials 9-1-1, it gets put on hold.

Stress can become a way of life. When everything's an emergency, then nothing's an emergency. But as long as you feel stressed, the fight-or-flight response remains active and you continue to rack up fees, interest charges, and over-limit charges on your body's credit card account. It's only a matter of time before these show up as chronic, severe, and eventually terminal health issues.

## Fear, Terror, and TBWCWS

Whether you're a freelance terrorist or a full-fledged government agency, when you want to manipulate millions of otherwise intelligent, reasonable people into giving up their rights, privileges and power, the most effective tool, hands down, is Fear. Fear calibrates at 100, and it's the perfect level of consciousness for controlling the masses. Fear prevents people from thinking for themselves, and puts them in a delightfully receptive state in which they're willing to believe anything or follow any suggestion, no matter how pointless or stupid, as long as it promises to make them feel Safe. At the same time, Fear has enough available energy so that the people can actually do the stupid, pointless things they're told to do. Below Fear, at the level of Grief (75), people stop thinking, but they lack the energy to take any action. Above Fear, at the level of Desire (125), people have the energy to take action, but they tend to ask inconvenient questions.

Fear would be the perfect tool for world domination if it weren't for one small catch. Fear is powerful only so long as it's new and unfamiliar. Over time, Fear loses its effectiveness due to a condition known as TBWCWS (The Boy Who Cried Wolf Syndrome). Fear triggers the fight-or-flight response only if you believe you're in imminent danger of death. The longer you experience Fear without actually dying, the less impact it has.

In response to the September 11 terrorist attacks, the newly formed Department of Homeland Security initiated a terror-watch-level color chart to justify why you can no longer bring toothpaste or bottled water through airport security. In the eight years the system was active, the threat level never dropped below Yellow (Elevated). After a few years, no one even noticed when it spiked up to Orange (High) or Red (Severe). Recent (allegedly thwarted) terror attempts barely made it through a 24-hour news cycle. In the absence of an actual event, threats and warnings no longer bother you because you're used to them. They're familiar, so they no longer make you feel unsafe.

However, not feeling unsafe is not the same thing as feeling Safe. All of the fear-mongering still drains the balance in your Safety Need Account and keeps you trapped in Victim Consciousness. Because you've been living there for so long, it's become normal to you, and you don't notice it. This is just the way the world is. You can't remember feeling any different, so you don't realize how wrong things are. You no longer believe that happiness is possible. The most you can hope for is an end to your suffering.

# Attachments:
# The Source of Suffering

Between Fear and Anger, you find Desire. And no, that's not the slogan of the latest celebrity fragrance (at least not yet).[2] Desire lives in the heart of Victim Consciousness, and when used skillfully, it's an even better tool for motivation and manipulation than Fear, because Fear eventually loses its potency, but Desire never does. With Desire, the more you get, the more you want. In sales and marketing, Desire is often combined with Fear, using a very effective carrot-and-stick approach. Fear, of course is the stick, while Desire is the carrot.

Desire is what fuels your quest for happiness. However, when you experience Desire from Victim Consciousness, you believe that the Source of your happiness is outside of you. You pursue the things that you want because you think that when you get what you want, you'll be happy. This story is *real*, but it's not remotely *true*.

If you're at all familiar with The Law of Attraction, you know that you attract things that match the vibrations of your thoughts. Well, the definition of "want" is "to lack," so every time you say "I want," you're saying "I lack," or "I don't have," and that's exactly what you get—the *lack* of whatever it is that you want. If you've read *The Secret* and are angry that you haven't manifested that new BMW, this may be one of the reasons why.[3]

---

[2] Charlie Sheen, when you're ready to get serious, I'm ready to come back to the negotiating table. But just so you know, Lindsay Lohan's new manager/parole officer has been texting me, and Naomi Campbell just sent me a basket of muffins and a new cell phone.

[3] Instead of saying "I want," you can say, "I would like," or, "I would love." These use power, not force, and are more likely to attract experiences that you actually enjoy.

Wants exist only in Victim Consciousness. Once you step into Second Kingdom and integrity, you no longer want anything; instead, you have *preferences*, things you would enjoy or appreciate. You want things only when you're not feeling Safe. This means that in addition to anything else, when you want something, you expect that getting it will make a deposit in your Safety Need Account. You believe that you cannot survive without getting what you want, and you create an **attachment** to the thing or experience. Attachments are the source of all of your suffering. They are what keep you anchored in the depths of Victim Consciousness.

Like everything else you experience in Victim Consciousness, creating attachments seemed like a good idea at the time. Let's say you receive a big bonus at work and make a big deposit in your checking account. When you make this deposit in your checking account, you also receive a big deposit in your Safety Need Account, and your ego notices it. Your ego reasons that if having money makes you feel Safe, then having *more* money will make you feel *more* Safe, so your ego creates an attachment.

Under normal circumstances, you receive deposits in your Safety Need Account from a variety of sources. As soon as you create an attachment, however, you begin to focus only on the specific channel of that attachment. This means you're no longer receiving deposits from the other sources. As a result, the balance in your Safety Need Account goes down, not up. Your ego flies into a panic. You need an immediate influx of Safety. Naturally, the ego directs all of its attention to the attachment, because it knows that has worked in the past. This strengthens the attachment which, in turn, makes you feel even less Safe (Figure 8).

When you are free from attachments, you can receive deposits in your Safety Need Account from many different and unexpected channels.

When you create attachments, you can only receive deposits in your Safety Need Account from the channel of your attachment.

**Figure 8: Attachments**

The only way to feel Safe is to let go of your attachments. However, you can't let go of your attachments until you feel Safe. Fortunately, there is an easy, effective way to meet your Safety Needs and restore the balance in your Safety Need Account.

# How to Meet Your Safety Needs

Meeting your Safety Needs is quite simple, because the truth is that you're almost always Safe. Unless you're in a life-threatening situation (such as being stalked by a serial killer or being robbed at gunpoint), you are Safe. All you need to do to experience this is to become aware of it. When you step into Victim Consciousness, you step out of "My Business," and either dwell on the past, or worry about the future. The past and the future are none of your business. "My Business" is the Present Moment.

The way to meet your Safety Needs is to become aware of the Present Moment. You do this with the **Present Moment Awareness Safety Meditation**.

## The Present Moment Awareness Safety Meditation

❖ Stop whatever you are doing, and take a few deep, cleansing breaths.

❖ If possible, find somewhere to sit or lie down, and then let yourself feel supported by the chair, floor, bed, or sofa.

❖ As you become aware of your body and aware of your breathing, feel your mind begin to quiet.

❖ Gently release your attachments to any thoughts, and simply observe any activity of your mind.

❖ As you observe your thoughts, notice how they naturally, easily and effortlessly seem to circle around, gently spiraling inward until they settle in the Present Moment.

❖ When you are fully present, consider the Truth that right here, right now, *in this moment,* you are completely Safe. If any thoughts come up, observe them without attachment. They will naturally settle back down into the Present Moment.

❖ Consider the Truth that right here, right now, in this moment, every one of your needs is met. In this moment, you *are* enough, and you *have* enough. You are completely, easily and effortlessly supported.

❖   Let your awareness rest on your breath. Let your mind quiet.
     And for a few moments, simply be. Simply experience what
     it feels like to be completely Safe and completely supported.

**Download free MP3s of this guided meditation at
www.GetAngryGetHappy.com**

# The Moment of Truth:
# What Is Happiness Worth To You?

It's time to ask yourself the tough question: Are you serious
about getting happy? Most people say they want to be happy,
but they're not willing to take action and make the changes
in their routine that will make it happen. Personally, I don't
care one way or the other. I've already got some of your money
(thank you!) and whether you follow any of my advice or not is
none of my business.

Happiness is a *process*, not an *event*. If you've done the work
of Phase 1, you're already on the road to feeling happy because
you're taking back your power. But to see real progress, you have
to do the work of Phase 2.

The work of Phase 2 requires that you dedicate 20 minutes a
day for 30 consecutive days to listen to a guided meditation. It's
a nine minute meditation, and all you have to do is sit quietly
and listen to it twice a day, morning and evening.

You have six different versions of this meditation to choose
from. One has just my voice; one has the sound of gentle
rain falling, and the other four have music at the beginning
and the end. You can download the MP3 files for free at
**www.GetAngryGetHappy.com**. These files are included as

bonus gifts if you bought the book from me online. Otherwise, all you have to do is create a free user account to download the meditations.

This is possibly the most important thing you can do to transform your life, take back your power, move out of Victim Consciousness once and for all, and become truly happy. All you have to do is be willing to invest 20 minutes a day.

You probably won't notice any big changes right away, but stick with the program. Soon, something will blow up in your life, and you'll notice it didn't create as big of a mess as it would have in the past. That's how you'll know it's working for you.

You'll always have the meditation files as a resource, but once you become familiar with what it truly means to feel Safe, you can do this exercise on your own in a matter of seconds. Whenever you notice the balance in your Safety Need Account dropping, you can restore it with the **Present Moment Awareness Safety Meditation**.

Until you feel Safe, you can't master your Anger. In order to master your Anger, you have to be able to *feel* angry without *being* angry. You also have to understand more about the nature of Anger, so keep reading. You'll learn about this in the next chapter.

# Chapter 7
# A Closer Look at Anger

**N**ow that you're feeling Safe, you're ready to take a closer look at anger. It's important to be able to identify anger correctly in the field; often what you experience as anger may be something else entirely. Once you know how to identify anger, you'll learn the difference between *being* angry and *feeling* angry. Finally, you'll address anger in your relationships, and what you can do about it.

## Is It Anger or Is It Impatience?[1]

Dr. David Hawkins has observed that much of the time, what we call anger is actually impatience. For example, when you're stuck in traffic and running late, or you're in a rush, and the driver in front of you insists on actually driving the posted speed limit, you're not angry, you're impatient. When you feel impatient, you're not in the Present Moment. You're projecting into the future, which is none of your business. All you need to do to feel better is take a deep breath and practice the **Present Moment Awareness Safety Meditation**.

If you are chronically impatient, you might find it helpful to repeat a mantra to yourself, such as, "My timing is divine."[2]

---

[1] Well?? Which is it? I don't have all day!!

[2] "…and my shoes are *fabulous!*"

You will get where you're going when you get there, and not a moment before. You do not have any control over the external circumstances that are causing you to be late. However, you do have control over how you feel when you arrive.

The feeling you experience when you don't get what you want when you want it is also probably impatience, rather than anger. The attachments you have to the want itself, and to the timing of getting that want, drain your Safety Need Account. The **Present Moment Awareness Safety Meditation** will restore the balance in your Safety Need Account. This can shift your perspective and allow you to find other, more effective ways to resolve the issue.

# Is It Anger or Do You Just Need a Snack?

In his book, *Healing and Recovery,* Dr. Hawkins points out that often what we experience as uncontrollable anger is caused by low blood sugar. Dr. Hawkins suggests that a great many people are functionally hypoglycemic, and when their blood sugar crashes, the result is feelings of anger, rage, and depression. When he was still seeing patients in his psychiatric practice, Dr. Hawkins insisted that new patients eliminate all sugar and alcohol from their diet. Over the years, about 25 percent of the patients were "cured" by the time they had their first appointment.[3] Dr. Hawkins recommends a book called *Sugar Blues* by William Duffy, which explores this phenomenon.

If you find that you're angry all the time and have a hard time controlling it, you might want to take a look at your diet and

---

[3] David R. Hawkins, M.D., Ph.D., *Healing and Recovery* (Sedona, AZ: Veritas Publishing, 2009), 265–266.

possibly get your blood glucose levels checked. As powerful as the **Present Moment Awareness Safety Meditation** is, it won't address the physical (and physiological) causes of your anger.

# Being Angry vs. Feeling Angry

If you're not impatient and you're not hungry, then what you're experiencing is actual anger. What you do about it depends on whether you *are* angry or you're just *feeling* angry.

When you *are* angry, you're in Victim Consciousness. Your dominant vibration calibrates at 150, the level of Anger. When you *are* angry, your "little r" reality is defined by and limited by Anger. This means that you will always *react* rather than *respond*. You will use force, and whatever action you take will make the situation worse.

When you *feel* angry, you experience the *vibration* of Anger, but you're not limited by the *consciousness* of Anger. Anger is a part of your "little r" reality, but it doesn't define it. You can *feel* angry without being pulled into Victim Consciousness, and this gives you the ability to respond (using power) rather than to react (using force).

The difference between *being* angry and *feeling* angry is Safety. When you practice the **Present Moment Awareness Safety Meditation**, you will gradually restore the balance in your Safety Need Account. The experience of Safety calibrates at 250 (the level of Neutrality). When you are able to maintain at least this level of consciousness, you can feel angry without also feeling unsafe. Anger will no longer automatically drain your Safety Need Account and catapult you into the heart of Victim Consciousness.

Please remember, this is a process, it's not an event. Getting to the point that you truly feel Safe is a matter of months, not days. Even so, all you have to do is be willing to invest 20 minutes of your time and listen to the **Present Moment Awareness Safety Meditation** twice a day. If you do this consistently, you will reach the stage when you can begin to master your anger. Once you are able to feel angry without feeling unsafe, you can harness the energy of your anger to help you to get happy. (You'll learn how to do this in Phase 3.)

# Anger and Other People: This Time It's Personal

Now that you understand the difference between *being* angry and *feeling* angry, it's time to look at the last major experience of anger: being angry *with* someone. Because, let's face it: the number one item on the list of things that have the potential to really piss you off is other people.

Other people are one of your greatest resources for anger. Why do you think you spend so much time in "Other People's Business"? When you step into "Other People's Business," you get to judge, criticize, blame, and generally feel smug and superior to other people. This has always been a great source of comfort to you... until now. Now, the Red Pill is really kicking in, and you're about to be hit with the most mind-bending, unexpected plot twist imaginable.

*There are no other people.* [4]

---

[4] I was hoping to have Rod Serling handle this reveal because it's worthy of *The Twilight Zone*. I was informed that he's not available because he's dead. I explained that I knew he was dead, and was hoping for a significant discount. I was then informed, that in addition to being dead, Mr. Serling was also not interested.

Every single person you encounter is a mirror. They're reflecting your own issues back to you.

This is what that quote in the Bible is *really* talking about. When it says, "Judge not, that ye be not judged. For with what judgments ye judge, ye shall be judged; and with what measure ye mete, it shall be measured to you again,"[5] it means that when you judge other people, you're judging yourself because other people reflect your issues back to you. It's really a fancy way of saying, "I'm rubber, you're glue. Whatever you say bounces off me and sticks to you."

No matter what the *reality* of the situation, the *truth* is that it's never about the other person.

I'm going to set this next part in big, bold type because it's really important to accept:

## You can NEVER control how any other person thinks, feels, or behaves.

Take a few minutes if you need it, and get over the shock of this massive paradigm shift. When you're ready to continue, I'll show you why this is a really good thing. Any resistance or discomfort you're feeling right now is showing up because even though you recognize the truth that **you can never control how any other person thinks, feels, or behaves**, there's a part of you that believes that you *should* be able to. And as long as you think that you *should* be able to control other people's behavior, you'll get pulled into Victim Consciousness.

This next bit is directed at the part of you that not only believes that you *should* be able to control how other people

---
[5] Matthew 7:1–2.

behave, but also believes that being able to control how other people behave would be a good thing.

Let's say, for a moment, that you *could* control how other people behaved. In other words, you had the power to make all of the people in your life relate to you exactly the way that you think they should.

Now, if it were possible to control other people, would it make sense that you would be the only person in the world who could do it? Of course it wouldn't. If *you* could control how other people behaved, then *everyone* would be able to control how other people behaved. That's only fair, right?

So, in order for you to have the ability to control how other people behave, then everyone would have to have that same ability. That means that while you could control how other people behave, other people could control how *you* behave.

Let's give that a try. Right now, go to your computer, log onto **www.GetAngryGetHappy.com**, and buy another copy of this book. But don't stop there. Max out your credit card and buy 5,000 copies of it. Do it now!

You see, if it were possible to control how other people behaved, then *I* could control how *you* behaved. And if I could control how you behaved, you would be giving me all of your money right now instead of thinking, "Go suck an egg."[6]

See? Not being able to control how other people think, feel or behave is a *good* thing.

But how does that stop other people from pissing me off (I hear you cry)? Well (I answer), all you have to do is look at your

---

[6] I'm paraphrasing, of course. If I revealed what you were *really* thinking, I'd lose the PG-13 rating of this book. Not to mention that even after years of Pilates, I'm just not that flexible. I could stretch for hours and I still wouldn't be able to go suck an egg. Not that I've ever tried.

relationships in a different context. For example (I continue, resolving to abandon this reckless use of parentheses), when someone pushes your buttons, you usually *react* and say, "Stop pushing my buttons!" When you try to stop others from pushing your buttons, you step into "Other People's Business," and it drains your Safety Need Account. Because **you can never control how any other person thinks, feels or behaves**, you can't stop people from pushing your buttons.

However, you now know how to manage the balance in your Safety Need Account. This means that when someone pushes your buttons, you have options. Having a button pushed doesn't automatically throw you into Victim Consciousness. Instead of *reacting* with, "Stop pushing my buttons!" you can *respond* and say, "Oh! I have a button!" Your buttons are your business. If you don't like having your button pushed, *get rid of the button*. Once the button is gone, no one can ever push it again.

## Getting Rid of Your Buttons

You're about to learn how to get rid of the most common buttons you have. Doing this will significantly improve every one of the relationships in your life. Now, obviously, there's more to improving relationships than just erasing your buttons, but that's a subject for a different book.[7] This book will address the buttons you create from your expectations.

In *Loving What Is,* Byron Katie talks about the origin of her process, known as The Work. She realized that all of the stress

[7] Specifically, it's a subject for *The Relationship Handbook: How to Understand and Improve Every Relationship in Your Life.* Check it out at www.TheRelationshipHandbook.com.

she experienced came from wanting reality to be different than it is. "When I argue with reality, I lose—but only 100 percent of the time."[8] Your stress, frustration and anger don't have anything to do with reality: they come from your expectations that reality should be different than it is. All you need to do to let go of your stress, frustration and anger is to adjust your expectations to match your reality. The Work of Byron Katie is a simple four-question process that is extremely effective in doing just that.

I'll share an example from my own life of how to get rid of a button. For the past few years, I've had a standing weekly coffee date with a dear friend. Now, being on time is very important to me, and I almost always get wherever I'm supposed to be at least 5 minutes early. I don't expect other people to do this, but I do expect that people should show up on time. This became a problem for me because my friend *never* showed up on time. No matter what time we agreed on, she was consistently 10 to 15 minutes late. I never made a big deal about it because even then, I was very conscious of staying in "My Business," but frankly, it was really starting to piss me off. What's more, my friend could see that it was pissing me off and that I was doing my best not to involve her. As a result, I know that she was making an effort to show up on time, even though she still showed up late every week. Now, we were both feeling bad about it.

Eventually, I realized that this was *my* issue and not hers. The problem was my expectation that she would show up on time. Obviously, my expectation was unreasonable, so I adjusted it to fit reality. I changed my expectation to expect that she would

---

[8] Katie, 2.

show up about 10 minutes later than the officially agreed on time (which she did). Now, when she arrives, I'm perfectly happy to see her. She no longer has to watch me try to hide my annoyance, because I'm no longer annoyed. By adjusting my unrealistic expectations, I made both of us much happier.

As simple as that example was, it's also a bit misleading because it makes the process look easier than it may be for you. The reason this example is so straightforward is that I always stayed in "My Business," so I only had to address my expectations. Expectations deal with actual behavior. When you get mixed up in stories about what that behavior means, or *why* a person is behaving the way they are, you encounter *judgments*. Just as **you can never control how any other person thinks, feels or behaves**, you also never can know what anyone else is thinking or feeling. *Why* someone behaves in a certain way is none of your business.

In *Transcending the Levels of Consciousness,* Dr. Hawkins points out that we're never angry with someone for what they *are*; rather, we're angry with them for what they're *not*.[9] For example, you're not angry with someone because they're stingy; you're angry with them because they're *not generous* (and you have an expectation and judgment that they *should* be generous). You're not angry with someone because they're rude, you're angry with them because they're *not polite* (and you have an expectation and a judgment that they *should* be polite).

When you're angry with someone, you will need to pick apart the story and uncover your hidden judgments and expectations about what they *should* do and why they *should* do it. You'll

---

[9] Hawkins, *Transcending the Levels of Consciousness:*, 143.

know that you've adjusted your expectations because you won't feel angry anymore.

In case it's not obvious, you have to feel Safe before you can do this process. You can't *be* angry and question your story. However, you can *feel* angry and look at your expectations as long as you also feel Safe. The minute you notice yourself getting angry with someone, stop and do the **Present Moment Awareness Safety Meditation**. Then, you can locate the buttons being pushed, adjust your expectations and judgments, and eliminate the buttons once and for all.

# The Anger Response

Many years ago, Rev. Guy Williams introduced me to the idea that anger is not a primary response. He said that anger arises because one of your expectations hasn't been met, but that anger is actually the *third* feeling you experience.

First, you experience Grief (which calibrates at 30), as you mourn the death of the expectation.

Next, you experience Fear (which calibrates at 100). You become afraid that things will never change, that this is the way things will always be, that your expectations will never be met, and that you will never feel Safe.

Finally, you experience Anger (which calibrates at 150).

Even though this process takes place in the realm of Victim Consciousness, it's quite powerful. It also demonstrates how you're wired to recover from the shocks and disappointments in life by automatically reaching for the best-feeling thought currently available. In a matter of seconds, you can move from the paralysis of Grief and Fear to Anger, where you can access enough energy to get out of Victim Consciousness and feel Safe once more.

This works only if you have mastered the energy of Anger and know how to use it as a springboard to jump out of Victim Consciousness and into integrity in Second Kingdom. Most people get stuck at Anger and react using force, which keeps the cycle of victim and victimizer going. The real value of Anger is that it has enough energy for you to become aware of your expectations and change them to be in alignment with reality.

If you don't address your expectations, you won't feel truly Safe. You'll continue to experience undercurrents of Grief and Fear, which will drain your Safety Need Account and keep you mired in Victim Consciousness. You'll step into "Other People's Business" and tell yourself that the other person *should* have behaved differently. The more you tell this story, the more painful and powerful it becomes, and each time you tell it, you *should* all over the place. Eventually, you end up with a big, steaming heap of *should*, which is exactly as unpleasant as it sounds.

The problem with big piles of *should* is that you never know when you're going to step in one and track it all over the carpet. The bigger the pile of *should*, the more likely something will remind you of the story, and then you'll have to spend the rest of the day scraping *should* off the bottom of your shoes.[10]

If you would like to get rid of all of that resentment and clean up all of the *should*, you're going to have to bring in the big guns. You'll have to resort to using the "F-Word."

---

[10] Don't even try to get it out of suede.

# The "F-Word"

The F-Word is a highly-charged topic. It's a cornerstone of many spiritual traditions, and there's no doubt about the good it can do. When used properly, it's the key to moving out of Victim Consciousness for good. The problem with the F-Word is that it's commonly misunderstood. Instead of helping people get out of Victim Consciousness, it keeps them trapped there.

You may be a bit confused right now, and if you are, it's because you're trying to figure out how any of this applies to the *other* F-Word. The F-Word *I'm* talking about is *forgiveness*.

The reason most people misunderstand forgiveness is that they think that forgiveness benefits the person being forgiven. This is not true. The person who benefits from forgiveness is the person doing the forgiving.

Let me illustrate with a story. Let's say that you're really, *really* angry with me. From my point of view, the fact that you're angry with me is none of my business. As long as I stay in "My Business," I will live a happy life in blissful ignorance of how you feel or what you think about me. Meanwhile, you are standing in the heart of Victim Consciousness, convinced that you can make me feel all of the pain, frustration and suffering that you're experiencing because you're angry with me. This, of course, is silly because **you can never control how any other person thinks, feels or behaves**.

You believe that you're punishing me because you're holding a grudge against me. Holding a grudge is exactly like drinking poison and waiting for the other person to die. As long as I stay in "My Business," I'm not being punished by your anger. Meanwhile, *you* are suffering—a lot. While you're stuck in Victim Consciousness, you see forgiveness as some prize that you get to withhold from me until you decide that I'm worthy of it.

The truth is that it's none of my business if you forgive me or not. If you do forgive me, it won't have any effect on me whatsoever; however, it will affect you in powerful ways. You'll stop telling the story, you'll stop living in the past, and you'll stop suffering.

# Pain (Unavoidable) and Suffering (Optional)

It's important to understand the difference between pain and suffering. You might think they're the same thing. This is another misconception that keeps you trapped in Victim Consciousness.[11] Pain is unavoidable; it's a part of life. To put it bluntly, pain happens. Suffering, on the other hand, is mostly optional.

Pain is experienced in the Present Moment. Pain is a *feeling*, and although for most people, it's not a pleasant or enjoyable feeling, it's still a feeling. The only appropriate response is to surrender and let it flow through you. Just like any other feeling, once you've felt it completely, it goes away, and you're done with it. What most people do when they experience pain is resist it; however, resisting pain makes it worse and prolongs the experience.

Suffering, on the other hand, occurs when you tell and retell the story of a painful experience. You suffer only when you drag the past into the present instead of letting it go. The past is none of your business. You have no power there, and you can't change it, so it's a part of Victim Consciousness. The only reason your

---

[11] Collect them all!

past has any influence on your present is that you keep carrying it with you.

There's an old story about two Buddhist monks on a journey. One was a senior monk, the other a junior monk. During their journey, they approached a raging river, and on the riverbank stood a young lady. She was clearly concerned about how she would get to the other side of the river without drowning. The junior monk walked straight past her without giving it a thought, and crossed the river. The senior monk picked up the woman and carried her across the river. He set her down, and the monks parted ways with the woman, continuing their journey. As the journey went on, the senior monk could see some concern on the junior monk's mind, and he asked what was wrong. The junior monk replied, "How could you carry her like that? You know we can't touch women, it's against our way of life." The senior monk answered, "I put her down at the river's edge a long way back. Why are you still carrying her?"

Traumatic, painful experiences immediately drain your Safety Need Account. If the trauma is severe, it can also change your "wiring" so that even after the experience is over, you continue to feel unsafe. Each time you tell the story or relive the experience, it drains your Safety Need Account again, reinforcing the pattern. Very quickly, you can forget what it means to feel Safe, and believe that this chronic lack of safety is all you will ever experience. It's essential that you stop telling the story, and instead practice the **Present Moment Awareness Safety Meditation**. Over time, this will help you to fix your "wiring" so that you can once again feel truly Safe. Whenever you find yourself reliving the memories or telling the story, stop and remind yourself of the truth that right here, right now, you are Safe, and you are *not in pain*. What you experience when you tell the story is *suffering*.

As long as you hold on to the experience and cling to your anger at the person or people who hurt you, you will remain trapped in Victim Consciousness. The people who hurt or abused you are responsible for the *pain* you experienced at the time. *You*, however, are responsible for your own *suffering*.

When someone harms you, it's natural to want that person to be punished. It's completely reasonable, perfectly understandable, and absolutely *none of your business*. It's not your business to enforce the law, and it's not your business what kind of justice or retribution someone else receives. Justice will always prevail, because that's the nature of the Universe.

The Universe is completely just; however, it's not always fair. When you've been hurt by someone, you're not interested in justice. You want fairness, which would involve making sure that they experience exactly as much pain and suffering as they caused you. Once that happens, *then*, you believe you'll be happy.

Even if you could personally punish someone for hurting you, it wouldn't be enough. It wouldn't matter if you could make that person go through exactly the same experience as you did, because **you can never know what anyone else is thinking or feeling**. There's no way to know that they're suffering the way you suffered. When you insist on justice, all you do is prolong your own suffering.

Don't be too hard on yourself, though. The only reason you chose to suffer was that you didn't have any other options. You were trapped in Victim Consciousness, and you had to console yourself with the meager entitlements you found there. These can lessen your suffering for a brief time, but they can't end it. But now that you know how to maintain the minimum balance in your Safety Need Account, you have a choice. You can move out of Victim Consciousness and end your suffering completely. You do this by practicing the **Present Moment Awareness Safety Meditation**.

When you start to feel Safe and have stepped out of Victim Consciousness, you can begin to unravel the story so that it can no longer pull you back in. First, you must be willing to dive into the heart of the story one last time, and allow yourself to feel all of the pain without resisting it. Be present with the pain, but avoid describing it or telling stories about it. Once you've truly felt the pain, it will be gone for good. Now, you can look at the story from a place of power and truth. When you take the story out of Victim Consciousness, it's no longer something that happened *to you*. What you will discover is that forgiveness is no longer necessary, because there's nothing to forgive. You can let go of the story completely. It no longer has any power over you.

From this expanded context where you access the power of the Present Moment, you can adjust your expectations. You can decide if or how you choose to relate to the former objects of your resentment. Since you are no longer tied to these people by your anger, you can finally release them from your life and have nothing more to do with them. Or, because you are free from your past and your old, unrealistic expectations, you can build a new relationship with them, based on boundaries and expectations that support you.

When you drop your old stories and stop suffering, you free yourself from your past. Who you were no longer limits or defines who you are, or who you can become. You will be amazed at how much more energy you have because you're no longer wasting it, reliving past resentments. For the first time in your life, you feel truly powerful.

Of course, once you have all of this freedom and energy you will be faced with a brand new challenge: What do you do with it? You'll figure that out in Phase 3.

# ANGER MASTERY

## PHASE 3

# Chapter 8
# The Value of Happiness

**W**elcome to Phase 3 of the Anger Mastery Process! The dedication you've shown in going to the gym, staying in "My Business," and of course spending a whole month listening to the **Present Moment Awareness Safety Meditation** twice a day is paying off. Not only are you feeling considerably less anger, you're also feeling considerably more happy—and from this point on, it only gets better.

How do I know that you've done all of this work? Because you're reading this chapter! If you hadn't done that work yet, you wouldn't be reading this far ahead.

Or would you?

I see. You're *that* sort of reader. Well, be warned, this chapter is full of super-secret security measures. It knows if you've been doing the work or not. It knows the balance in your Safety Need Account.[1] And if you haven't been doing the work, or you don't have a sufficient balance in your Safety Need Account, all of the words in this chapter will automatically translate into some language you can't read, like Mandarin, or Sanskrit. Or Klingon.

You are being scanned now…

Scanning…

---

[1] It does not, however, know if you've been sleeping or know when you're awake. This is a book on Anger; it's not Santa Claus.

Scanning…

Scanning…

Scanning…

Scan complete.

Okay, maybe I was exaggerating a little bit. Remember how expensive it was going to be to include actual Red and Blue Pills in the book? Well, that turned out to be pocket change compared to what it would cost to translate the rest of this chapter into Klingon. If you're reading this on a Kindle, however, and you didn't do the work in Phase 1 and Phase 2, it will become gibberish.[2]

But seriously, if you haven't done the work of Phase 1 and Phase 2 for at least a month, this chapter won't do much for you. It may make sense to you on an intellectual level, and when you finish reading it, you'll *know about* how to become happy. However, you won't *know* happiness, and you won't become happy. If reading about something was enough to change your life, you'd be thin, rich, and have the sex drive of a 20-year-old. And even though this chapter might not translate into Klingon, how much you get out of it depends on how Safe you are.

It's none of my business if you read this chapter right away, or if you do the work first. I've already got some of your money because you bought the book (thank you!). But as you do the work, move out of Victim Consciousness, and begin to feel truly Safe, I invite you to read this chapter again. You'll be amazed at how different it is each time you read it. The more Safe you feel, the more you'll understand. You'll be able to use more of the techniques you'll learn in this chapter, and using the techniques in this chapter will help you to get very happy, very quickly. But

---

[2] The gibberish feature will be included in the next upgrade.

to be absolutely clear, **none of the techniques in this chapter will work for you unless you are able to maintain a healthy balance in your Safety Need Account and stay out of Victim Consciousness**.

That's why this chapter is Phase 3, not Phase 1. You have to learn to crawl before you can run.

## Clearing Out Your First Kingdom Storage Units

The purpose of Phase 1 and Phase 2 of the Anger Mastery Process is to help you to move out of First Kingdom/Victim Consciousness. When you complete these phases, your primary residence will be somewhere in Second Kingdom. You will notice that you are considerably happier, and that your life flows with greater ease because you use power more than you use force. The more familiar you get with your new neighborhood, the less time you'll spend visiting First Kingdom.

But you know how it is when you make a big move. You're so busy shopping for new furniture that you don't have time to get rid of the old stuff, so you rent out a storage unit and resolve to go through it later. You did the same thing when you left First Kingdom and moved to Second Kingdom, except your First Kingdom storage unit is filled with the beliefs, stories, and judgments that ran your life while you lived in Victim Consciousness. It doesn't matter that you're enjoying your shiny new beliefs and stories in Second Kingdom; as long as your old beliefs are still in that storage unit, they will drain your energy and limit how happy you can feel. In Phase 3, you will slowly and methodically clean out your First Kingdom storage unit by pulling out one belief, judgment, or story at a time, taking it back with you into Second Kingdom, and releasing it.

It's critical that you have a full balance in your Safety Need Account before you begin this work. When you start to pull things out of your First Kingdom storage unit, you will uncover all sorts of negativity, including Grief, Fear, Anger, and Pride. You will need to stay present, so that these feelings do not drain your Safety Need Account. If the balance in your Safety Need Account gets too low, you won't be able to leave First Kingdom.

If you know exactly what you're looking for before you make the trip to First Kingdom, it limits the amount of time you have to spend in Victim Consciousness. You can facilitate this by asking yourself three Big Questions.

# Big Question Number 1: What Do You Want?

The first Big Question is, "What do you want?" If you're still spending most of your time in Victim Consciousness, this question makes no sense. It's not a big question. It's barely even a question. In Victim Consciousness, your life is focused on survival. Everything you want, you want in order to feel Safe. You never have to ask what it is that you want, because you always know what you want, and there's never enough of it.

Once you feel truly Safe, however, things change. For the first time in your life, you have choices and options that aren't limited to the question of survival. Now, "What do you want?" is a much bigger question.

Even though you're standing in Second Kingdom when you ask, "What do I want?" the answers come from First

Kingdom. Specifically, they come from your First Kingdom storage unit. Make a list of the things that you want. Then pick one for closer examination, and move on to the *next* Big Question.

# Big Question Number 2: Why Do You Want It?

On one level, the answer to this question is obvious. The reason you want *anything* is that you believe when you get what you want, *then* you'll be happy. Even though getting what you want has never made you happy before, a part of you still believes getting what you want is the secret of happiness. It lives in your First Kingdom storage unit, and you're about to evict it.

Now that you live in Second Kingdom, you know that your happiness doesn't have anything to do with getting what you want. In Second Kingdom you understand that the reason you want things is that you believe that getting what you want will make a deposit in one or more of your Need Bank Accounts. In Second Kingdom, you believe you'll be happy when all of your needs are met, and you know you can meet your needs without getting what you want.

If you *want* something, that means you have an attachment to it, so first and foremost, that want has to do with meeting your Safety Needs. You know from the work you did in Phase 2 that the only effective way to meet your Safety Needs is to practice the **Present Moment Awareness Safety Meditation**. So, do that now.

Seriously.

I'll wait.

Now that you're feeling Safe, think about what it is that you wanted. You may be surprised that you no longer care about it as much. It would be fine if it just showed up, but now that you feel Safe, it may not be worth the effort to go out and get it. If you no longer care about the thing you wanted, congratulations. You've just cleared out an old item from your First Kingdom storage unit. You're one step closer to becoming truly happy. Select another item from your list of wants, and repeat this step.

On the other hand, you may still care about the thing that you wanted. Because you've let go of your attachments to it, thinking about it probably feels a lot better now than it did before. This means that getting what you want would also make a deposit in your Validation Need Account or your Self-Actualization Need Account. It's no longer about getting something; instead it's about a feeling of accomplishment, appreciation and self-esteem. You care about this intention because it makes you feel good about yourself. You may also care about it because of how you think it will make other people feel about you.

Whoops! That last part is none of your business!

If a big part of your motivation to accomplish something is based on how you think it will make other people feel, you have to ask yourself whose happiness you're working toward. When you question why you want the things you want, you may discover that you never wanted those things in the first place. You wanted the things you wanted because those things were important to your parents.

I'm going to save you years of therapy. A good portion of your life has been spent trying to live up to your parents' expectations, because you believed that when you met those expectations, your parents would love you, and *then* you'd be happy.[3] Everyone has some version of this in his or her First Kingdom storage unit. These beliefs supported you as a child, but now that you're an adult, there's no reason to keep them.

When you lived in First Kingdom, your happiness was all about getting what you want. Now that you've moved into Second Kingdom, your happiness is about meeting your needs. Meeting your needs has a much higher rate of happiness than getting what you want, but it's still possible to meet all of your needs and still not be happy. The real secret of happiness is staying connected to your *values*. And this brings us to the last Big Question.

# Big Question Number 3: Do You *Really* Care About What You Care About?

This is a *really* Big Question. In fact, it's one of the biggest. It may not be quite as big as questioning the meaning of life itself, but it's pretty close: It questions the meaning of *your* life. If you haven't developed your safety muscles and aren't feeling completely Safe, asking this question can have unpleasant consequences.

When you ask this question, you may discover that you've spent most of your life pursuing things you don't actually care about. Your immediate reaction probably will be to beat yourself up. Please don't (unless you're into that, in which case, knock yourself out[4]). Until this moment, you couldn't have known the things you wanted wouldn't make you happy. You had to

---

[3] And that's all the time we have for today. Yes, the hour really flies by when it only lasts 50 minutes. You can schedule your next appointment with the receptionist. And remember: I don't validate you, so why should I validate your parking?

[4] Metaphorically, not literally.

live your life pursuing those things to find out. You have not been wasting your life. Now that you know the truth, you're free to look for things that you truly care about. Pursuing those experiences *will* make you happy.

What you're questioning here are your *values*, and this is what Phase 3 of the Anger Mastery Process is about. You need to identify the value systems that run your life, and get rid of the value systems that you don't, well, value. You're about to discover that your First Kingdom storage unit mostly contains other people's values.

## Evaluating Your Values

Think of values as articles of clothing. It doesn't matter how well they fit the department store mannequin; all that matters is how well they fit you. When you were growing up, you didn't have much say in your values. You had to make do with the values you parents gave you. Sometimes these fit, and sometimes they didn't. And sometimes they embarrassed you so much that you had to change into something more acceptable before you got to school so you wouldn't get laughed at.

As you got older, you were exposed to the most popular value systems of the world. It's impossible to miss them, because they're advertised everywhere. They all look so stylish and cool that you can't wait to try them on yourself.

You know how the quality of your clothing depends a lot on where it was manufactured? Well, the same thing goes for your values. Almost all of the popular values that you encounter in the world were proudly manufactured in First Kingdom. These include valuing money, success, control, influence, fame, and sex, to name a few. All of these values promise happiness, but they don't ever deliver.[5]

There's nothing inherently wrong with any of these values. Some may not be appropriate for you because they don't suit your style or flatter your frame. Other values may be a good start, but just like with clothes, you can't expect a perfect fit when you buy off-the-rack. You have to be willing to make alterations. You alter your values by questioning what it is about a particular value that really matters to you.

Questioning your values strips away the external, unnecessary parts. What you're left with is a Core Value. Your Core Values are the key to experiencing lasting happiness.

# Discovering Your Core Values

Your Core Values include one or more of these: **Abundance, Balance, Beauty, Freedom, Harmony, Joy, Love, Order, Peace, Power, Unity,** and **Wisdom**. The first thing you may notice is that these are abstract, eternal qualities. These are the qualities of the Universe, and they are present in everything at all times. For example, it's not possible for you to run out of **Beauty** and have to go down to the corner store to pick some up; **Beauty** is always present. All you can do is fail to notice it.

Your Core Values represent feelings and concepts that come from Third Kingdom. This is why they feel wonderful and represent the true path to your happiness. Because they're part of Third Kingdom, however, they're nonlinear, and beyond form. They can't be described with words, because words are part of Second Kingdom. Words are only a jumping-off point;

---

[5] Plus, they fall apart the first time you wash them.

you have to *feel* these Core Values for yourself. It's the difference between reading a detailed description of an apple, and taking a bite of one. Needless to say, you can't experience your Core Values until you truly feel Safe.

You can discover your Core Values by questioning the things that you want. It's easiest to start with an actual *thing* that you want, say, a new car. Begin by getting in touch with the feeling of wanting that new car. Visualize the experience of having the car, and everything that it would involve. Picture yourself enjoying the car completely. Now, ask yourself what it is about that experience that you most appreciate and enjoy? Which Core Value best describes it?

For example, when you think about your new car, you may picture yourself driving along the coast, well above the posted speed limit, with the top down, the stereo blasting, and the wind in your face. What is the essence of this experience for you? It might be **Freedom**, or it could be **Joy**.

Or, when you think about your new car, perhaps you picture yourself leaving your house in the morning, seeing your car in the driveway, and taking that few extra seconds to admire it. You might look forward to spending weekends washing and waxing your car and keeping it absolutely spotless. For you, a new car might be an expression of **Beauty**.

Because wants come from First Kingdom and represent force, they always create a counter-force. This means that whenever you want something, it's related to something else that you *don't want*. Sometimes it's easier to discover your Core Values by looking at what you *don't want,* instead of what you want, and picking the Core Value that is the *opposite* of that experience.

For example, you may want a new car because you *don't want* to keep dealing with the stress of your old, unreliable car. You *don't want* to wonder if your car will start in the morning. You *don't want* to get stranded in the middle of the night, waiting for a tow truck. What you *really don't want* is to feel helpless and impotent. For you, manifesting a new car might be an expression of **Power**.

Once you choose a Core Value that feels good to you, start paying attention to it. Look for the presence of that Core Value in every situation, and discover how it's always been the real reason that you go after the things you pursue. The more you connect with and open up to the experience of your Core Value, the more happiness you will experience. Your life won't be about the destination anymore, because you'll enjoy the journey itself. When you connect with your Core Value, you discover that the Source of your happiness is within you, right here in the Present Moment.

## Abundance as a Core Value

You may look at the list of Core Values and immediately say that **Abundance** is what you care about the most. This would probably mean that you didn't complete the work in Phase 2, and you're still operating from Victim (and Lack) Consciousness. Here's how to check. When you think about **Abundance**, do you think about an abundance *of* anything (like time, money, freedom, power, love, etc.)? If you do, then you haven't discovered your Core Value; you've discovered an attachment. Go back and practice the **Present Moment Awareness Safety Meditation**. As you begin to feel truly Safe, the attachment will fade, and you'll be able to discover what you really care about.

The people who do have **Abundance** as a Core Value are out feeding the world and discovering new sources of cheap, renewable energy. They are called to celebrate and demonstrate the infinitely abundant nature of the Universe, and nothing about that abundance has anything to do with their personal resources. **Abundance** as a Core Value is rare; I've yet to meet anyone with it, personally.

Remember, it doesn't matter what anyone else thinks, feels, or values. The objective is for you to discover what *you* truly value and how it feels to *you*, because that's what will lead you to becoming truly, eternally happy.

## That's Nice, But What Do I Do Now?

You may not appreciate it yet, but the information in the past few sections is absolutely essential to your happiness. Unfortunately, it's also some of the most challenging and difficult information in this book, especially if you haven't done the work of Phase 2 (and you were translating it from Klingon). All I can say is that the more you do the work, the more sense it will make to you. In the meantime, let's get practical.

Right now, having done the work, you've got lots of energy and more freedom than you've ever had, and you don't know what to do with it. When you lived in Victim Consciousness, all of your energy was devoted to getting the things that you wanted so you could survive. This energy is different. This energy is yours to play with. You get to use it to create, to express yourself, and most of all, to have fun.

Chances are, you have no idea how to do this. First of all, when you lived in Victim Consciousness, you didn't have the time or energy to have much fun, let alone to create. Plus, the value systems you used to live by didn't support you in staying connected to the spark of your creativity. That spark is still there inside you, however.

Think back to the dreams and interests you had growing up. What did you enjoy? Art? Music? Dance? Cooking? Is there a musical instrument gathering dust in your attic? An old paint set and an easel in your basement? A pair of tap shoes in your closet? Turn off the television and spend some time getting reacquainted with them. Take a class. Practice. But most importantly, do it for *you*.

Way back in the olden days when there were only three television networks and all of the news fit into 30 minutes a night, people had hobbies. Hobbies were how you spent your free time. (This was back when people actually had free time.) Hobbies were fun (at least for the hobbyist) and that's what mattered. People built model airplanes, or collected stamps, or played bridge, or gardened. Some people performed in community theater, others made pottery or knitted. Hobbies provided a creative outlet and offered a sense of personal fulfillment that is sorely lacking in the world today.

Whatever hobby you choose, if you enjoy it, you can be certain that it is helping to connect you to your Core Values. Your hobbies can also help you to meet your Self-Actualization Needs, because they help you to grow and expand as an individual. While you're always looking to improve, for the most part, hobbies aren't competitive. It doesn't matter what anyone else is doing, or what anyone else thinks of your efforts. The only records you care about breaking are your own.

This, however, flies in the face of some of the most prevalent and popular values of modern society. Before you can take up a hobby and truly enjoy it, you may need to clear out a few more things from your First Kingdom storage unit.

# Fame: What Is It Good For?[6]

We live in a culture that worships celebrity. Our collective values have gotten so twisted that most people would prefer to *be* a personality than to have one.

The ultimate dream of Victim Consciousness is to become rich and famous. In today's climate, of course, becoming rich is out of the question. That particular club is not accepting any new members. However, thanks to the unlimited supply of reality television and talent competitions, it's possible to become *famous*, and cling to the slender chance that being famous might eventually allow you to become rich. It certainly improves your chances of *marrying* rich. Of course, if you're *really* famous, the rich part won't matter, because everyone in the world will love you, and then you'll be happy.

Remember, your perception of fame comes from First Kingdom. No matter how attractive it seems, the fine print will get you in the end. There's an entire genre of reality television devoted to documenting the downfall of people who became exactly as famous (and temporarily as rich) as you dream of being, and the one thing it didn't make them was happy.

The obsession with fame and celebrity has more subtle and damaging effects, however. More than anything, this is what limits and suppresses your creativity. These First Kingdom

---

[6] Absolutely nothing. Uh-huh.

values are what make you care about what other people might think of your creative efforts.

Who cares if you've got any talent for art? If you enjoy painting, paint. Play music because it feeds your soul. The more you practice, the more you'll improve, and the more you'll enjoy it. But don't do it because you dream of touring with your favorite band or winning *American Idol*. Don't do it for fame, or validation from other people. Do it because it's *fun*. Do it because it feels good.

**What anyone else thinks of your creative efforts is none of your business.**

Strive to become an artist, not a celebrity. Take classes, explore new things, learn and grow for *you*. Don't worry about making a living while doing these things. You don't have to. Work your job (or jobs) and recognize that your job is not who you are; it's how you support who you are. If this seems impossible or unreasonable to you, you're not feeling Safe enough.

There's nothing wrong with being an amateur singer, or a novice musician. Go sing at a karaoke bar, or in your church choir, or even in the shower. Get together with some friends and rock out in your garage. If the neighbors complain, you can all chip in and get it soundproofed. Find something creative that you enjoy, and *go enjoy it.*

This, like everything else, will take practice. Your friends and family may encourage you[7] and tell you how you should open your own gallery, or shop your demo, or audition for *America's Got Talent.* Accept the compliments and enjoy the validation, but be careful not to buy into their First Kingdom values. The

---

[7] Well, your *friends* may encourage you.

minute you pick up those old values, whatever you're doing stops being fun. On the other hand, the more you explore your creativity for its own sake, the happier you will be.

# Lather, Rinse, Repeat

Mastering your anger is a *process*, not an *event*. Anger is a valuable, powerful resource. Learning how to use the energy of your own anger has two important benefits. First, when you master your anger, you can use the energy of your anger to get happy. Second, when you master your anger, other people can no longer steal your energy or manipulate you into doing stupid things. However, it's not enough to go through the Anger Mastery Process once. You have to keep repeating it for optimal results.

Thanks to the Anger Mastery Process, when you begin to feel angry, you have options. Most people get angry and get stuck in Victim Consciousness, but you can apply the Anger Mastery Process and use that energy to get happy.

First, identify whose business you're in and step back into "My Business."

Next, use the **Present Moment Awareness Safety Meditation** to refill your Safety Need Account.

Finally, take the energy of your anger and direct it toward something constructive that has nothing to do with the situation or person which made you angry in the first place.

The more you work the program, the easier and more automatic it becomes for you. You'll begin to store up the energy and be able to use it when you need it instead of having to get rid of it all right away. Gradually, your experience of your "little r" reality will transform. You'll feel more free, more powerful, more creative, and most importantly, more happy than you've ever felt before.

I think that's worth the $9.95 you paid for this book, don't you?

So what are you waiting for? Get angry! Get happy!

# ANGER MASTERY

# APPENDIX

# Appendix
# Resources and
# Recommendations

**H**ere you will find some recommended reading that will help you with the Anger Mastery Process. In particular, you'll learn more about Dr. David R. Hawkins and The Work of Byron Katie. You will also learn how you can schedule a personal consultation with me, if you're so inclined.

## Dr. David R. Hawkins

Dr. Hawkins is an internationally renowned psychiatrist, physician, researcher, and pioneer in the fields of consciousness research and spirituality. He writes and teaches from the unique perspective of an experienced clinician, scientist, and mystic, and is devoted to the spiritual evolution of mankind.

The collected writings of Dr. Hawkins represent the highest level of spiritual truth in the English language. As life-changing and transformational as his books are, they are not, on the whole, easy to read. If you are interested in learning more about the science of consciousness research and the Map of Human Consciousness, I recommend you start with either *Transcending the Levels of Consciousness* or *Healing and Recovery*.

*Transcending the Levels of Consciousness* is a comprehensive journey through the "little r" realities of each of the different calibrations on the Map of Human Consciousness. I personally find it one of the most readable of Dr. Hawkins' books, although his style may take some getting used to. If you're completely new to Dr. Hawkins and would like to begin with this book, start by reading the Biographical and Autobiographical Notes at the very end of the book. This will introduce you to Dr. Hawkins and give you a context that will make reading the actual material much easier.

*Healing and Recovery* is the easiest of Dr. Hawkins' books to read because it's transcriptions of lectures, so the language isn't as dense. The focus of this book is, obviously, on all types of healing. However, it will familiarize you with the fundamental principles of consciousness, which will make his other books more accessible.

Visit Dr. Hawkins' website at **www.VeritasPub.com**.

# The Work of Byron Katie

If you find that you're having difficulty letting go of your stories, especially stories about how other people are behaving in your life, Byron Katie can help. The Work is a simple process—only four questions—that will help you to release your judgments, drop your story, and move into integrity. Katie's books consist mainly of transcripts of her taking people through this gentle, loving process. The only recommendation I have for you is that this process will be much easier, and far more powerful if you make sure you're feeling Safe before you use it, so start with the **Present Moment Awareness Safety Meditation**.

Learn more at **www.TheWork.com**.

# Consultations With Kevin B. Burk

If you prefer the personal touch, I am available for private consultations either in person (if you happen to be in the San Diego area) or via telephone. Although I work with clients around the world and cover a broad range of issues, the main focus of my work is to help my clients to become happier. I offer astrological and spiritual counseling, as well as relationship coaching, and what I call "spiritual training."

If you're really serious about transforming your life (and you're willing to do the work), I have a program called **Archetypal Astrology: The Hero's Journey**, which will help you to Become the Hero of Your Own Story.™ Learn more about it at **www.TheRealAstrology.com/HERO/**.

You can request a consultation through my astrology site (**www.TheRealAstrology.com**) or the Anger Mastery site (**www.GetAngryGetHappy.com**).

# About the Author

**K**evin B. Burk has been helping people around the world to improve their lives and relationships since 1996 through his astrological counseling and relationship coaching practice. His humor, wisdom and compassion are always present in his books (ten so far, including *Astrology: Understanding the Birth Chart* and *The Relationship Handbook: How to Understand and Improve Every Relationship in Your Life*), his classes and workshops, and his interactions with his clients and students. Kevin's focus is always on the practical, exploring how we can actually use astrology and spiritual practice on a daily basis to transform our lives.

In the astrology world, Kevin is best known for making Classical Astrology accessible to everyone, taking complex and abstract concepts and showing how they can be used to create concrete, specific, and practical interpretations. Kevin's astrology website, **The Real Astrology with Kevin B. Burk (www.TheRealAstrology.com)**, is one of the premiere astrology resources on the Internet, hosting well over 2,000,000 visitors since its launch in 1996. His first book, *Astrology: Understanding the Birth Chart* (Llewellyn, 2001) was used as a textbook at Kepler

University in its Undergraduate Astrology Degree program, has been translated into Russian, and is currently being translated into Bulgarian. Kevin's articles have appeared in *The Mountain Astrologer,* the Australian publication *Well Being Astrology,* and in *Llewellyn's Moon Sign* annuals. His "Ask Kevin" video clips have a loyal and growing following on YouTube and Facebook.

In the nonastrology world, Kevin is best known for his revolutionary approach to understanding and improving all human relationships through **The Relationship Handbook** and **The Relationship Workshops**.

Kevin has recently released a series of DVDs on his Law of Attraction workshops: **Prosperity & The Law of Attraction,** and **Astrology & The Law of Attraction**.

Kevin can be reached at Kevin@GetAngryGetHappy.com or by phone at 619-807-2473.

www.ingramcontent.com/pod-product-compliance
Lightning Source LLC
Chambersburg PA
CBHW071005040426
42443CB00007B/663